# Brain Respiration

Hyndae Intelex Bldg., 261 Nonhyun-dong Kangnam-ku, Seoul, Korea
Tel : 82-02-3218-7531, Fax : 02-3218-7519

# Brain Respiration

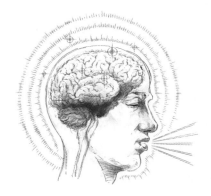

HAN MUN HWA

# Contents

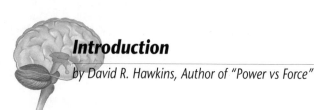

# Introduction
by David R. Hawkins, Author of "Power vs Force"

This work is a valuable contribution on 3 levels. 1) It creates an understanding of Ki-energy and how to use it for improved health, well-being and ultimately enlightenment itself. 2) It is a practical instruction manual on how to move the Ki-energy to best advantage. 3) It is a report by its author of the subjective shift from identification of the I-self with illusory local and limited temporality to a non-local and unlimited universality—the I of the real Self. The statistical chances of experiencing the phenomenon called "enlightenment" is approximately 1 in 10 million persons and its rarity therefore makes such subjective reports valuable to the world at large, not especially to the spiritual student.

The spiritual student has numerous obstacles to overcome : Firstly, the attachments and illusion of the ego. Secondly, the magnetic influence of the entire field of human consciousness and the programming of the mind that ensues. Thirdly, the student is actually engaged in a process of jumping the time frame of evolution. The first two obstacles are well covered in the spiritual literature. The third has not really been specifically addressed and therefore deserves some comment.

The biological evolution of the human brain is still at a quite rudimentary and primitive level. The egotism and vanity of mankind leads to its overestimation of the present capacities of the human mind. In fact, however, the human mind and brain are grossly defective and function mostly in a desultory faulty and unpredictable style.

The majority of mankind staggers on in such a haphazard manner that the average business person is lucky if they remember to take the keys to the office with them in the morning. Quiet desperation or a transitory happiness based on ignorance and denial are the lots of the average person whose life is devoted primary to physical, financial and emotional survival.

Our society is characterized by high rates of crime, divorce, drug use, criminality, mental illness, suicide, death by accident or disease, bankruptcy, obesity and emotional turmoils that range from "road rage" to an epidemic of depressive illness. ( 30 million people are on Prozac )

Most people live lives based on regret, resentment, fear, anxiety, worry, insecurity or greed, avarice or hatred and revenge. In between the above they dwell in endless hours of remorse, guilt, shame or intoxication and mindless escapism such as gambling, overeating or the endless acquisition of material possessions, pride and gain. The mass entertainments of rock-music, brutal sports and escalated forms of mayhem such as TV murder and war are the narcotics that ensure continued unconsciousness. The continuous assault of the senses by violence or seduction dulls the populace's capacity for discernment.

In my own research on the nature of consciousness which was reported in the book, Power vs Force, The Hidden Determinants of Human Behavior (Veritas, 1995) I wrote that the consciousness (Cs) level of 85% of the world's population calibrates below the level of integrity (the level of 200 on a scale of levels of Cs which goes from 1 for physical existence to 600 as the level of enlightenment). Only 0.4% of the world's population ever reaches the level of love (at 500). The Cs of the average person advances only 5 points in a lifetime. Thus the whole of the population when stratified according to levels of Cs is like a pyramid with extremely few individual at the top and the great mass of mankind below the level of integrity.

Let us recontextualize the position of the human brain in an overall scale of biologic organ evolution. The kidney or liver for instance are many millions of years old in evolution—they function extremely well under even severely adverse conditions. I jokingly tell people that you have to practically beat them to death to make them stop working—They even go on for a period of time after a person is pronounced dead. The human brain, in contrast, only recently appeared in evolution. It "forgets", "feels bad", gets embarrassed, makes mistakes, miscalculates and misfunctions most of the time. Let us look at one simple fact that it itself is so overwhelming that few people have the humility or brilliance to appreciate the full impact of just one basic observation—the human brain and mind at this point in evolution lack the innate capacity to be able to tell truth from falsehood! That is a staggering realization and explains the whole human dilemma throughout history, from war to famine, disease and poverty.

Every individual is deluded and believes his/her view of what is "real" is valid. In reality most people haven't the slightest idea of what runs their life or is even responsible for their continued survival. Were it not for the innate Wisdom of Ki-energy/Spirit factor, which is the basic energy that expresses itself as life, no one would have survived long enough for their ego to take credit for it.

I have taken some time to present all of the above so as to prepare the basis for the most crucial jumping off point for all spiritual evolution : humility. Without that primary quality no real spiritual progress can occur and self-delusion with pseudo-spiritual content is the common result. Thus, I was impressed and pleased by the commitment of the Dahn Meditation Centers and Il Chi Lee in finding easier and more effective ways to lead people to real spiritual progress. What all these mutually helpful efforts mean to me is that there is an enormous human thirst for truth and spiritual advancement. Because everyone whose Cs advances benefits all of mankind, to support and further this process deserves our greatest respect and support.

My own personal experience of the process reported

by Il Chi Lee was similar. After a prolonged period of severe anguish (the dark night of the soul—which can go on for many years) I surrendered at great depth and to a drastic degree "walked off the cliff" in that final moment of unbearable agony. Suddenly, without warning, what I had always thought of as my "self" disappeared and was replaced by an Infinite Presence of all things showed forth in self-revealing brilliance which was the infinite power of omniscience shining forth as manifestation. The Self as the true source of all existence both visible and invisible was so stunning that the mind fell permanently silent on that day in 1965 and was replaced by a infinite silence in which I had to learn how to speak again and how to go about ordinary business as the human motivations were obliterated and replaced by the all encompassing Presence.

Enlightenment is not an intellectual understanding. It is an amazing experience, sensationally vivid, of becoming one with the cosmic energy. An energy of sublime joy and pleasure flowed ceaselessly up my back and into the brain. The experience of the flow was intensely pleasurable and would fluctuate in locality in my brain to wherever I focused my attention. Later the energy would run down over the forehead and into the chest and heart. It would radiate forth from the heart unbidden to perform healings and miraculous events all on its own. These had nothing to do with, nor did my overall state, any personal self. The world believes that the remaining personality which learned again to venture forth and do the work of the world is an individual person like themselves. This is an illusion brought about by the projection of the separateness of their own ego-self. No such entity exists. Cs itself speaks and acts for its own evolution and welfare which includes everyone by virtue of its very nature. All of mankind is slated eventually for enlightenment and the efforts of each of us to hasten that process are supported by the Divine Will.

The teachings of Il Chi Lee are in themselves an expression and manifestation of the Ki-energy of the Self extending forth into the world. It is for that reason that the Self expressing itself as existence wrote at the end of the report of such experience, "Gloria in Exelsis Dio" for there are no more accurate words to describe the realization of the Self. That which is Il Chi Lee's, Ki is not different from that energy which shines forth in its expression as the universe and all that is in it.

This is indeed therefore an important and praiseworthy book for it helps us get close to the truth and actual experience of our own reality as the Self which transcends all of time, which always was, always will be, before and after all worlds or universes.

*David R. Hawkins, M.D., Ph. D.*
*Director, Institute for Advanced Spiritual Research*
*Sedona, Arizona August 1997*

# Preface

Since the end of the Twentieth Century, scientific knowledge of human brain function has expanded enormously. The human brain is no longer a mysterious black box to modern people. The information revealed by current brain research is no longer an exclusive concern for a few scientific experts. Rather, the subject is becoming more and more popular with non-technical people who want to know more about themselves.

There is no other way to human self-understanding except through the brain. The brain is where human thoughts and emotions are produced. Recently, we discovered that the amygdala, which is located just underneath the cerebrum, controls human emotions. If this part of the brain were to be eliminated, a person would totally lose emotional responses. Since human emotions are the workings of the memories stored in the amygdala, one can solve emotional problems by purifying the amygdala. Based on this new information about the brain, we can approach a lot of our mental dilemmas from a totally different perspective. When we unveil the secrets of our brain, we can possibly understand humanity better. Such knowledge will help to find the solutions for the individual and social problems which seem to have been with us forever.

Brain Respiration is based on the knowledge that by transforming our brain, we can direct our physical/mental/ emotional transformation. There are many secret buttons inside the human brain which control our physical, mental and emotional activities. Problems develop when some of these secret buttons are broken or are out of working order. Brain Respiration is designed to fix these broken buttons to recover their functions and thereby, to restore people to their original state of perfection - physically, mentally and emotionally.

Many people are suffering from many kinds of diseases. Despite our scientific successes, there are still undiagnosed, incurable diseases. Most of our diseases are initiated by mental and emotional disturbances. This is why the health of our brain is so important, because the brain is the delivery room for our mental and emotional activities.

Brain Respiration is a special way of breathing which makes the brain active by means of "Ki" —Korean expression for Bio-energy or power of life. Through Brain Respiration we can activate the blood and energy circulation, thereby bringing more oxygen into our brain. By activating the circulation of the blood and energy, we can find remedies for most of the diseases in our modern society. Particularly, Brain Respiration has great effects on releasing stress and rediscovering a peaceful mind, on preventing dementia, and on alleviating overeating.

Heavy stress in our modern society is the most threatening symptom shared by almost everyone. Stress is literally the root of every modern ailment. Unfortunately, even if we become aware of this negative force of stress, only partial treatments are available. There is no final solution, yet.

Furthermore, the development of modern science continually increases the average life span, making it longer than ever before. Due to the growth of the aging population, fear about the typical infirmities of the aged grows stronger than in previous generations. For example, the fear of dementia, "the AIDS of the aged," is more widespread than ever before. Dementia destroys the basic ability for survival along with the personality, and the victims become an unbearable burden for the rest of the family. This problem becomes more serious in developed countries, where the percentage of the population of the aged is often higher, due to life extension.

Despite our highly developed modern technologies, war and starvation still threaten us. The power of modern technology is sometimes used for destroying and killing, rather than serving people. Development of more and more dreadful military armaments diverts time, money, and technology away from finding more efficient ways to feed people and cure their illnesses. The brutality of human beings seems to be increasing, thereby inhibiting the entire progress of civilization. Why do we have to repeat the same insanity again and again, even when we so well know the dangers stemming from this regressive attitude?

It is crystal-clear now that modern science is no longer capable of healing our problems. The sharp blade of scientific reason and analysis has failed to cut off the deep roots of our problems. Science, the God of the Twentieth Century, is no longer capable of keeping its throne. We urgently need to find a different approach to our current dilemmas.

With such an awareness of the limits of modern science, people start to question the effectiveness of intellect. The recent increasing interest in EQ(Emotional Intelligence Quotient) and MQ(Moral Intelligence Quotient) is, thus, more than a trend. It reflects popular distrust in the western concept of intelligence which shows itself most vividly in IQ. Up to this time, the left brain has been predominant in society and IQ has been the first marker of an individual's ability. The left half of the brain is certainly a deciding factor in producing an egocentric and competitive personality. Now, we need to move on toward a right brain society, where EQ is accepted as more important for creating a harmonic and creative personality. Furthermore, we eventually hope to build a society based on a high level of MQ people, who have enlarged their consciousness to such an extent that they want to contribute to the well-being of the whole of humankind.

These days we hear not a few people raising their voices to emphasize the importance of EQ and MQ. They strongly feel both the necessity and responsibility to end the tragic drama which seems to drive human history to self-destruction. In addition to that kind of realization, what we need now desperately is a practical solution or aid. These were the ideas that motivated me to write this book : Brain Respiration.

Brain Respiration is a special way of breathing, to restore the whole brain functions and thereby to help us meet the true self hidden in the depth of our existence. It is a very simple and effective way of elevating EQ and MQ, and will make, I'm sure, a great contribution to the recovery of our humanity.

Brain Respiration has its origin in Dahn Hak, the Korean traditional discipline for training body and mind. Dahn Hak is supposed to have begun about 10,000 years ago. Such a long time ago Korean ancestors practiced it in their daily lives. They did not pursue a selfish well-being of their own, but shared the same noble aim to realize their ideal potentiality and benefit humankind. They knew that any kind of individual well-being is an illusion : no living thing can exist even just for a moment without the cooperation of all the other living or non-living things. Dahn Hak was a way of training themselves to reach the ideal of life in harmony with nature.

Dahn Hak leads us to complete self-awareness by feeling and utilizing Ki, the source of life. This exercise puts a great importance on correct breathing. Through breathing, we can control the flow of Ki in our body. Through breathing, we can enter the world of our mind and realize the universal principle inherent in various phenomena of nature. It improves our natural healing power and our body becomes filled with a fresh life energy, which naturally cures our physical and mental diseases.

When I was a young man, I wandered for a long time, in a desperate hope to know the true meaning of being and life. After going through deadly strict self-discipline, I experienced the fundamental energy of the cosmos and then realized that the cosmic mind is none other than my own mind. I learned that any living thing is healthy when it is in the great flow of cosmic life.

Later, I found that all my discoveries were already summarized in the Dahn tradition. Thereafter, I put all my efforts toward modernizing and systematizing this ancient tradition for contemporary people. Currently, in Korea, we have established 300 centers all around the country, with over 100,000 members. Many people do Dahn Hak every morning in over 1,000 parks all over the country. It is such a joy and pleasure to witness people rediscover their health and find the true meaning of their lives.

I have been sharing this precious tradition with people throughout the world for the past 3 years. I came to America to teach Dahn Hak to the American people. We now have 30 centers in the United States, and more centers will soon be open. Currently, I am living in Sedona, Arizona, the world famous city of the sacred and the beautiful. I have many plans to share Dahn Hak on a wider global scale with many other peoples all over the world.

Brain Respiration is the essence of Dahn Hak. Through Brain Respiration, we can get to the core of our existence, and there, we will have a wider view and deeper insight. We will touch the unlimited world of possibilities, which lies hidden inside of each of us. Very often the human brain is compared to a computer. It is true that up to this time, we have only touched the peripheral part of this wonderful device and have never yet entirely used the main part of it. No one can estimate what capabilities we could have when the silent part of our brain starts working. Someday, in the future, we may consider our current brain function as a rather primitive one.

After I attained enlightenment, I felt deeply that you and I are not two but one. I realized that all things of the universe exist as one. From then, I came to look upon the problems of humankind as mine. The pains of humankind are my pains, and the crises of humankind are my crises. Humankind is now struggling to find a new exit, passing through the end of the tunnel of the 20th century when all the attempts of the civilization face their serious limits. I am convinced the age-old and timeless exercises of Dahn Hak for the perfection of human beings will show the light of great hope and possibilities.

I pray that these Brain Respiration exercises will contribute to your health and happiness. Thank you.

*Il Chi Lee*
*from Sedona, Arizona. May, 1997*

# 1. The Basic Structure and Function of the Brain

# A. Imagination, the most advanced function of the brain

Even though contemporary scientists have gone far in revealing many secrets of the human brain, with all the available help of modern technology, we still do not know to what extent and directions we can utilize our own brain. People say that we use only a very small part of our brain's potential ability however hard we try. Even a genius like Einstein is said to have used only 10% of his brain's abilities. We do not yet know what kind of capabilities the other unused 90% of the brain has.

One effective way we might utilize our brain more than 10% is to practice applied creative imagination. When we use our imaginative power, we could possibly integrate the other 90% veiled part of the brain. Imagination, as the most advanced function of brain, is the only tool we have to explore the unknown world of our brain.

Then, how does the imagination affect our body? How does the information stored in the brain affect humans?

One of the American medical research centers conducted an experiment with prisoners sentenced to death, in order to discover the relationship between one's imagination and one's body. The result was quite surprising. The research team visited a prison and asked the death penalty prisoners whether they could assist in their medical research project. The project was about measuring how much blood is shed, until one reached death. Researchers suggested that any volunteer for the experiment would have $1,000,000 paid to the family. Researchers described in advance the whole procedure of the experiment. "We will cut the four arterial blood vessels in your wrists and save your blood in a container. We will constantly check the amount of blood in your body to see when you lose your consciousness, and when your heart stops. However, you will be put under local anesthesia, so there will be no pain."

There were three volunteers. The research team put the

prisoners on a bed and tied up their arms and legs. They showed the whole operational setup and then blindfolded the volunteer's eyes. In this situation, the research team portrayed a plot, telling the volunteers that they cut the artery vessel on their left wrist, and then pretended to do so with the dull edge of a knife. The prisoners were filled with fear and could not realize that the researchers were not actually cutting their blood vessels. Instead of blood, a sound was created with drops of water. Doctors screamed, "Press harder on his heart to get more blood."

In the experiment, without shedding one drop of blood, the three volunteers were dead. This is an example to show how our brain works. The death-sentenced prisoners died simply because they believed that they would die. As such, depending on what kind of information is put in the brain, the body can show a dramatic chemical transformation. The information controls your hormone secretion. Whatever is supplied to your brain, is taken in and then responded to by the brain. It does not matter whether the information is true or false. The brain simply accepts the data as it is. Therefore, if someone's brain receives information without any doubt and trusts it, it is possible that the information will be manifested into an apparent reality.

Recently, there was a very interesting article in a Korean newspaper. In a ward where the paralyzed patients were hospitalized, a huge snake stole in. As soon as the patients saw the snake, all of these paralyzed patients suddenly stood up and ran away from their beds. At the moment when they felt threatened, they forgot the fact that they were paralyzed. A strong survival instinct sent a message to their brains that they had to flee to the outside, and so it happened.

Everybody experiences more or less the same kind of situation to a different degree. For example, you may sit in a car which is parked. Suddenly, the car beside you starts to move, then you feel as if your car is moving and are surprised. If you happen to stop your car on the hillside, your illusion can be a big shock. You may scream and get nervous, because you think that your car is sliding down the hill. As such, once information is put into your brain, your brain responds to it, regardless of the truthfulness of the information.

In this sense, imagination is not just a phantom. Imagination has its own power to bring what is imagined into reality. The key to utilizing the imaginative power is believing. When you innocently trust the power of imagination, what you imagine will become real exactly as you imagined.

The world of imagination belongs to the world of the fourth dimension. In the fourth dimension, a spontaneous transition is possible. In fact, I saw a person who transmitted his sickness into a pine tree through the imagination and lost 5kg of his weight in a second. Our brain uses about 90% of its available capacity in the fourth dimension and only 10% in the third dimension. Ninety per cent of the brain is used in the fourth dimension only when you have a firm belief in that dimension.. When we start to utilize 90% of our brain in third dimension, we won't know what kind of human history will open up to us.

Brain Respiration is an exercise designed to utilize our imaginative power as fully as possible. Brain Respiration uses the imaginative power to exercise the brain and to transform it. See how your imagination can transform your life through practicing Brain Respiration.

# B. Scenic Landscape in the Brain

Human beings have the highest ratio of brain's weight to body weight among all the animals. The human brain is 1,500g, a whale's is about 800g, and an elephant's is about 5,000g. When we consider the ratio between body weight and the brain's weight, the human brain is the heaviest—1/40, compared with 1/2,000 of a whale and an elephant.

The human brain is so soft and delicate that it is easily damaged. Therefore, there are three layers inside the skull, as well as the skull to protect it. Also, the liquid inside the skull helps to prevent any direct shocks.

The weight of the brain averages only 2% of the whole body weight. The size of the brain is about the size of a small watermelon. However, the world of the brain is so profound and vast, that it is nearly impossible to comprehend its vastness. There is an unlimited world inside your brain, which can cover the whole scale of the universe. This is why people call the brain a "micro cosmos".

You do not necessarily need to have any professional knowledge about the human brain to do Brain Respiration. Nevertheless, a little acquaintance with the scenic landscape in the brain will help your practice. So, let's now take a trip inside the brain. The important thing is not to have some abstract knowledge, but to have the ability to visualize your brain. Imagine an anatomical picture of your brain is in front of you like a map and you are now going to visit each part of your brain's map.

First of all, let's go to the cerebral hemisphere, which is the largest part of your brain. The cerebrum is the latest development of the human brain. It looks like a walnut without a shell. The cerebrum is divided into two halves, the right and the left, and both sides are interconnected with each other by the corpus collosum. The corpus collosum is a bridge which allows an intimate relationship between the right and left halves of the cerebrum.

Look at the wrinkled surface of the cerebrum. The surface called the cortex of the cerebrum is the spot where our highest mental activities, such as thinking, judging, and creating, are accomplished. Thus, there are 140 billion nerve cells located there. Compared with other animals' brains, the highly evolved cortex of the cerebrum is the major distinction of the human brain. The lordship of all human beings originated from the development of the cortex of cerebrum.

There are many grooves on the surface of the cerebrum. Major grooves divide the cortex of the cerebrum into 4 lobes : the frontal lobe, the parietal lobe, the temporal lobe, the occipital lobe. The frontal lobe, the front part of the cerebrum is the largest one which manages language activities. The parietal lobe, the upper part, has to do with movement. The temporal lobe, the side part, has to do with the ear. The occipital lobe, the backside, relates to the eye. Thus, if you have any trouble with the backside of the brain, you will usually have some trouble with your eyesight.

# Cortex of Cerebrum

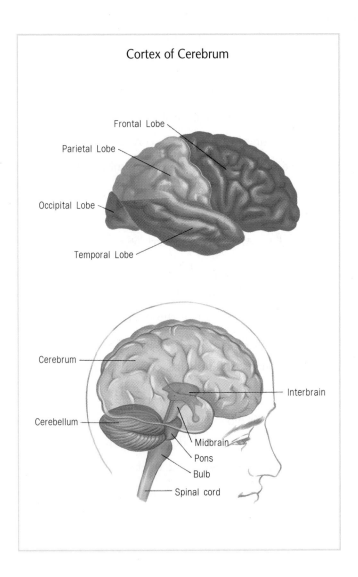

Frontal Lobe

Parietal Lobe

Occipital Lobe

Temporal Lobe

Cerebrum

Interbrain

Cerebellum

Midbrain

Pons

Bulb

Spinal cord

Now, let us go to the cerebral limbic system, which is underneath the center of the cerebrum. This part of the brain is related to our earlier development and is fully covered by the cerebrum. This area controls the human emotions and natural instincts. If the cortex of the cerebrum is the source of thoughts, the cerebral limbic system is the source of emotions.

A particular component of the cerebral limbic system is the amygdala. After the discovery of the function of the amygdala as the source of human emotions, many people became interested in that hidden part of our brain.

Next, we have the part of the brain called the cerebellum. The cerebellum is located under the backside of the cerebrum. The cerebellum has two parts, right and left, which have many horizontal grooves. The cerebellum has to do with balancing your body.

Now let's explore more deeply into the cerebrum and the cerebellum. In between the cerebrum and the cerebellum, there is the interbrain. Sagittalis, which takes up four-fifths of the interbrain, can be defined something like "a waiting room" (from the Latin). In other words, sagit-

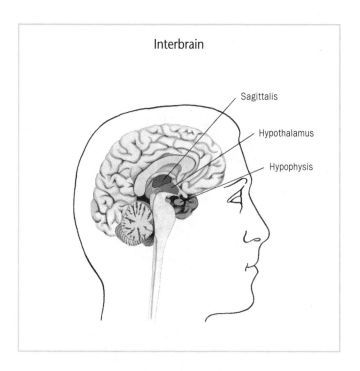

Interbrain

Sagittalis

Hypothalamus

Hypophysis

talis is a waiting place for sensory information where all information is collected first, before being distributed.

Under the sagittalis, there is the hypothalamus. At the hypothalamus is located the hypophysis. Hypophysis looks like a small bean. It is a place where many different kinds of hormones are produced. The hypothalamus is in charge of controlling our internal homeostasis, such as blood pres-

# Neuron and how to transmit information

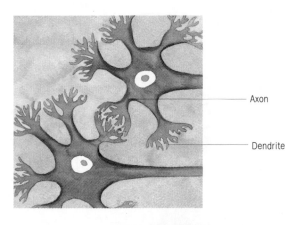

Axon

Dendrite

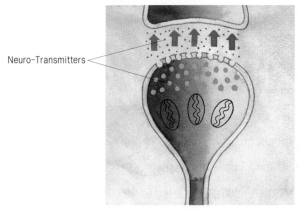

Neuro-Transmitters

sure, body temperature, blood sugar rate, stomach acid, water retention, and so on. If your blood pressure is too high or your body needs more water, it is the hypothalamus that makes your blood pressure lower and supplies enough water for the body. In short, the hypothalamus regulates our body in an appropriate condition to sustain our life. Also, the hypothalamus controls the hypophysis, as well as the appetite and sexual drives. If this part of the brain is damaged, you lose the sense of fulfillment and could suffer from excessive hunger and sexual desire.

If we go further down from the interbrain, there is the midbrain under the interbrain. Under the midbrain, there is the bulb. The midbrain is in charge of eye movements, such as the constriction of the iris, eyeball movements, and so on. The bulb is related to the most necessary physiology, such as the heartbeat, breathing, and digestion.

There are three parts of the brain, the interbrain, the midbrain, and the bulb, which are referred to as the brain stem. Before humans developed a more highly functioning thinking brain, the brain stem was a major part of the brain and enabled us to be alive.

Even though one's cerebrum or cerebellum is damaged, one will not die. However, if one's brain stem is damaged, it is difficult to escape death. When the brain stem is still working to keep one's heart beating and one's lungs breathing even if the cerebrum or cerebellum has been damaged, we call a person in this state a human vegetable. If one's brain stem is paralyzed and one can only breathe through an artificial respiratory machine, we call them brain dead.

The final visit on your brain journey is to the spinal cord, which is located at the bottom of the brain. It looks like a thin, long white cylinder. The spinal cord is a path for the motor nerves, sensory nerves, and the autonomic nerves. There is some spontaneous physical response to stimulation from the spinal cord. For example, if someone hit your knee, your calf would move up and down.

As we finish our brain journey, let us closely observe the brain cells. If we look into a brain cell closely, there is a nerve cell called a neuron. A neuron is composed of a star-like cell body, an axon and dendrites. One end of the cell body is attached to a long axon, which sends information to other neurons, and the other end of the cell body is attached to many dendrites. The dendrites, connected with an axon of a neighboring neuron, receive information. The juncture of axon and dendrites is called a synapse. A neuron is connected to thousands of other neurons through synapses.

At the end of an axon are a lot of pouches containing chemicals. When information is transmitted from one neuron to the other through a synapse, the pouches burst and the chemicals move. These chemicals are neuro-transmitters. If the neuro-transmitters don't function properly, some problems happen in the brain, which can cause mental diseases. For example, schizophrenia results from excessive secretion of dopamine, a kind of neuro-transmitter.

Up to now, we have briefly looked over the brain. I hope that you will store this basic information about the human brain inside your brain not by words but by pictures, and that you can make the landscape of the brain, if necessary, appear instantly in your head.

## 2. What is Brain Respiration?

# A. What is Brain Respiration?

If you stop breathing only for a few minutes, you cannot survive. Even though we are normally not very conscious of our breathing, breathing is quite an essential and basic vital activity for our survival. You may be able to endure a number of days without food, but are not able to survive without breathing.

Among all parts of your body, the brain is the most sensitive to breathing, or more exactly, the supply of oxygen. The human brain is a far more refined and complicated device than a highly upgraded computer which can carry on all sorts of complex and detailed tasks, and therefore the brain's activities need a lot of oxygen. Literally every activity we perform is interrelated with the brain.

Therefore, the part which consumes the most energy in our body, is the brain. The brain is only 2% of the whole body weight, about 1,500g., but it requires 15% of our blood, and even in a state of resting, the brain consumes 20-25% of the oxygen taken in by inhalation.

Blood circulation is quite crucial for the brain. If the blood supply into the brain is stopped for 15 seconds, we become unconscious. If it stops for four minutes, there will be some serious damage to brain cells. Because of this, there is a security system for the arteries into the brain; there are four major arteries which are very closely inter-connected with each other. In case of an emergency when one or two artery vessels are blocked, the blood can be supplied into the brain through the other arteries.

Then, what would be an easy and effective method whereby we could secure intake of more oxygen for the brain, other than normal breathing? There is a unique technique to supply more oxygen to the brain cells by activating blood circulation of the brain: Brain Respiration. Our natural breathing is an unconscious response to the difference between the pressure of the atmosphere and that of the lungs. Compared to this process, Brain Respiration is a more conscious level of breathing, which uses "Ki" as the source of life energy. Therefore, you need concentration, imagination, and most of all, the sensation of the "Ki" energy flow. Brain Respiration is a kind of breathing meditation for the brain.

When we say breathing in Brain Respiration, it implies a different meaning for breathing. In Brain Respiration, breathing does not simply mean taking in oxygen and releasing carbon dioxide out. In Brain Respiration, breathing means constant interaction with the source of life, cosmic vitality. When you inhale, you breathe in not only oxygen but also the cosmic energy for all life.

"Ki", this cosmic vitality, is the true essence of every creation in the cosmos. In the Orient, people have known of "Ki" for thousands of years and have utilized it in various ways. Oriental medicine, which heals people by correcting the distorted energy flow in their body, is an excellent example of this knowledge.

The vitality, Ki, taken in by inhaling, reaches into each cell of your body and makes it fully alive through recharging your body cells with fresh energy. During this energy recharging process, dead cells are burned off and new cells are formed. This is the circulation of life—taking in the fresh vitality and releasing out the used and aged energy.

As we see, through breathing, there occurs a constant interchange of energy between our body and the surrounding space. Here, we can summarize that the true meaning of breathing is to keep your body in vital aliveness by interacting with the source of life, the cosmic energy—the "Ki".

The major characteristic of this energy breathing, is that it is possible to do a concentrated breathing for any individual part in the body. If you breathe while concentrating on a certain part of your body, the energy in the body converges on that particular spot. Such a concentrated energy process has a powerful healing power which will completely boost our natural immune system.

Brain Respiration is a way of breathing to keep the vital energy concentrated on the brain. You are sending the fresh cosmic energy into the brain through respiration. This respiration process also makes the brain do exercise by use of this vital energy—the "Ki". Thus concentrated vital energy can vibrate your brain cells and lead them to expand and contract rhythmically. This movement awakens and re-activates each of the brain cells and thereby corrects any defect of the shape and function of the brain. In the process of this correction, one may hear an explosive sound in the brain.

As explained above, Brain Respiration is a way of breathing using the vital energy, Ki. Therefore, before you start to practice this breathing process, you need to recover the "Ki" sensation, first. The Ki sensation is derived from the concentration of your consciousness. We call this energy developed from concentrated consciousness "Jin Ki". which means the pure essence of our vital cosmic energy.

We can differentiate bio-energy into three different types :"Won Ki", "Jung Ki", and "Jin Ki". "Won" means "innate", "Jung" means "stamina or strength", and "Jin" means "true or genuine" in Korean.

"Won Ki" means the energy given by parents, "Jung Ki" the energy given by diet and breathing, and "Jin Ki" comes from the pure consciousness or cosmic consciousness. Won Ki has to do with our bodily construction, which is decided mostly by our inherited genetic information. Jung Ki is an energy source derived from food and respiration, which needs to be constantly refilled for healthy bodily functions. Therefore, Won Ki and Jung Ki are both limited sources of energy, because these two energies last only for a certain period of time. Jin Ki is the essence of all energies. It can only be generated through deep concentration of your consciousness. More precisely, Jin Ki develops when Jung Ki is combined with and empowered by the powerful waves your mind produces when you concentrate.

As Jin Ki is an energy generated by concentration, you can control this vital power with your own will power. If you concentrate on your hand, you will feel the energy in your hand. If you focus on your brain, the energy goes to the brain. When you concentrate, you can feel the heat in the exact spot where you focus your awareness. Once you feel the heat, you can prove the action of Jin Ki by measuring the temperature of the spot. You will find <the temperature of the spot, concentrated on> to be higher, than the other parts of your body.

Because Jin Ki comes from your mind, the quality of the energy varies depending on the state of your mind. There are different levels of Jin Ki. Breathing is important in that it enables the level of Ki to get higher. When you breathe in a state of deep concentration, which leads you to feel the flow of energy in the universe, you can produce Jin Ki inside your body and elevate your energy level.

Also, we can say that there is a pure energy and an impure energy. When we are in illness, it means that we have more impure energy than pure energy. Then, how is such impure energy formed?

The quality of our energy is determined by what kind of mind we have. As an example, our emotions are forms of energy. Love, peace, hatred, jealousy, anger, possessiveness, greed, selfishness, pride··· all of these emotions are different forms of energy. When we hold on to negative emotions, impure energy is stagnated in our body. Impure energy has a tendency to become stagnant, rather than freely circulating. Therefore, this dirty energy blocks the normal circulation of your energy flow and eventually creates imbalance and disease.

In this respect, the purpose of breathing is to circulate and recharge our energy. It is for eliminating impure, used energy and receiving fresh vitality, which purifies our whole bio-energy system. It is the same with Brain Respiration. Through breathing with our consciousness concentrated on our brain, we can take in the fresh vitality and transmit the energy to every cell of our brain. This will fully activate the brain and make it maximally healthy.

Once again, I want to emphasize that what is important in Brain Respiration is to feel the sensation of Ki through your body by controlling the Ki energy with your mind.

At first, you concentrate only on exhaling. You do not need to focus consciously on inhaling. Once you exhale, inhaling happens automatically, due to the difference between the pressure of your lungs and that of the atmosphere. When you can control your exhaling more naturally, you can do the same when inhaling, without any more effort.

The energy coming into your body through your inhaling process is transformed into Jin Ki, by the power of your mind. This energy reaches the brain by exhaling, circulates throughout the whole brain, and revitalizes each brain cell.

In short, Brain Respiration is breathing by means of Ki while deeply concentrating on the brain. Ki is generated from the mind, and circulated and controlled by the mind. Thus, in order to control your Ki flow, you have to control your mind. In other words, Brain Respiration is breathing through the mind.

# 3. The Purpose of Brain Respiration

# A. The Brain Needs Movements

Have you ever thought about your brain seriously up to this time? Have you ever thought about your brain as an organic living being?

Most of us normally do not think about our brain seriously except when we have headaches or wish we were smarter. Today, even though methods of right brain development have become more popular, and more public attention is being given to the brain's dysfunctional symptoms such as depression or dementia, people still do not see those issues as their own, unless they are forced to consider their own dysfunction.

In general, people share a fixed idea about the brain, and see this organ as the mysterious black box which is beyond their control. Because of such mysterious and awesome feelings about the brain, you may even forget that your brain is a part of your whole body. Also, it is believed that once your brain has fully matured as an adult, nothing can ever possibly happen to correct any defects or bring any changes in your brain.

However, we have to understand that there is a nerve circuit called the synapse. The synapse's primary function is to deliver excitement to the brain nerves. Synapses can be newly created and enriched, or degenerated, as the case may be, at any time, depending on the situation. If you use your brain, the branches of synapses are increased and strengthened, or vice versa, decreased and weakened from lack of use. The more stimulation into your brain there is, the smarter your brain function becomes. Furthermore, new experiences stimulate the formation of new synapses. In other words, new experiences can reformulate your brain.

Now it is clear that our brain is not a fixed entity, but an organically living being in the constant process of transformation. As you may know, this continuous change is the very nature of life. In Brain Respiration, what we mean by the transformation of our brain is the conscious restructuring of the brain by our own free will. It does not mean the natural alteration, like the aging process. Therefore, before we start to learn about Brain Respiration, we need to think about the brain as a friendly part of our body, instead of a mysterious black box.

Just as your muscles and joints get stiff and inflexible if you do not use them, the same thing happens to the brain ; if you use only certain parts of your brain, the other parts get harder, eventually becoming atrophied. Also, the constant tension created by emotional stress, will ultimately serve to constrict the brain. In order to make a stiff body flexible and more effectively functioning, we must practice exercises. The same is true with the brain. In order to keep your brain healthy and young, you need to do some exercises intensively focused on your brain.

The rigidity or stiffness in your body means that the energy flow in any particular spot is not very good. If the energy flow is not effective, neither is the blood circulation. The major reason for any blockage in the energy and blood circulation, is stress. Certainly, stress is the source of every discomfort we experience in life.

If we are stressed, our energy flow becomes blocked and stagnated. Eventually the whole energy course in our body becomes impure, and then, it is very difficult to take in any fresh vitality. In a state like this, our body is tense and stiff. On the other hand, being relaxed means that the circulation of our Ki is free and natural. When our energy flow is like that, it releases all the tension in our body, which makes us feel in peace and harmony. The reason we want to do Brain Respiration, is to reach this total state of relaxation both in body and mind.

Just as the blood needs blood vessels as a road for circulation, Ki also needs its paths to go around in the body. We call those paths meridians. Neither Ki, nor these meridians are visible to the eyes. If we can consider Ki as a train, and the meridians as a railroad, then the acupressure points in the body are the junctions of the railroad. The body' s acupressure points are like holes, where the Ki is coming and going. In other words, Ki is interacting with our body through acupressure points. When Ki is flowing through your meridians, it stays at the acupressure points for a while, and then, travels deeper into the internal organs.

If Ki flows freely and circulates smoothly, we are healthy and energetic. But, if it is not freely flowing, we become weak and ill. In general, blockages happen from the acupressure points first.

In most of the cases, modern people's acupressure points and meridians are clogged with impure energy, just as the blood's circulation is blocked by cholesterol. As the blocked blood circulation causes high blood pressure or heart attacks, the impure energy blocks the acupressure points and meridians. This weakens and disturbs the energy status, and makes the body vulnerable to stress and diseases.

Brain Respiration is a breathing process which leads the Ki energy to circulate in the brain. Brain Respiration, in highly concentrated consciousness, opens up the blockages in the energy paths in the brain. By breathing consciously, you can send fresh vitality and blood into the deeper regions of the brain.

Do you happen to know that the aging of the brain cells

is one of the key causes of dementia? People over thirty lose over 10,000 to 20,000 brain cells a day. Brain Respiration is a superior way to prevent the aging of your brain cells, through supplying fresh vitality into the brain. Most brain-related diseases are caused by malnutrition of the brain cells, or the serious constriction of the blood vessels in our brain. This also tells us how important the fluent circulation of blood and energy is in the brain.

Through practicing Brain Respiration, we can stimulate the circulation of Ki and the blood in the brain, which helps to restore the wholesome state of your brain. Because the brain is the main control center of all your bodily systems, a brain in good health makes sure that it's body is in optimal state. This is the first purpose of Brain Respiration.

# B. For A Peaceful Mind

Another purpose of Brain Respiration is to attain a quiet and peaceful state of mind by developing $\alpha$ brain-wave. As you may know quite well, a brain wave is an electric vibration that the brain emits when its nerve cells work. There are four different types of brain-wave ($\alpha,\beta,\delta,\theta$) according to the pattern and frequency the wave takes. Depending on the state of our mind and consciousness, the vibrational speed varies. When you are relaxed and feel comfortable, $\alpha$ wave ( 8-12 Hz ) is produced. Due to the extremely technological society in which we exist, most of us suffer from constant mental tension and anxiety. Presently, due to these technological stresses, various kinds of artificial aids to change your brain wave have been developed and are gaining increasing popularity. Also, more people are paying attention to practicing meditation, because it is known to lower brain waves. The effect of meditation on the brain wave has been scientifically proven.

The difference between Brain Respiration and other meditative techniques, is that Brain Respiration is a far easier method for you to master concentration, because it is based on the natural sensation of the bio-energy flow. Once you fully focus on the sensation of the Ki in your body and follow its flow with your consciousness, your brain waves come down without any effort. In such a state, everyone feels genuine joy, with much peace in his/her heart.

When you practice Brain Respiration, the drop of the brain waves is the work of Ki. As I described before, the human emotions are a form of energy. The various negative emotions, such as selfishness, jealousy and pride produce negative energy in our body. Such negative energy makes your mind shady and insecure. Negative and impure energy has a tendency to be stagnated, instead of being circulated. Therefore, once you are caught by these negative emotions, you cannot escape from them even by will, because the impure energy produced by those emotions holds you in a trap. The reason why people regain a peaceful mind after Brain Respiration, is that through Brain Respiration, we eliminate impure energy and replace it with pure energy

Feelings of instability and anxiety also have to do with the state of the Ki flow in one's body. If your abdomen is cold and your head is heated, your energy flow is reversed. The ideal energy flow in the human body is supposed to be like this : the cold, water energy comes up to the head, and the warm, fire energy goes down into the Dahnjon. The Dahnjon is the energy center in the abdomen.(See page 156) The water energy originates from the kidney, and the fire energy from the heart. When your head is cool and your Dahnjon area is warm, your energy circulation will be normal and healthy. We call this "Su Song Hwa Gang" in Korean. When your energy flow is natural and clear, as with Su Song Hwa Gang, there is a lovely peace in your mind.

If your energy flow is reversed, your Dahnjon is cold and your head warm. In that case, you would have a headache with other symptoms of feeling uneasy in your chest and, at the same time, suffer from indigestion because the temperature of your internal digestive organs gets too low.

By practicing Brain Respiration, you can correct the reversed energy flow in your body. Once you recover the state of Su Song Hwa Gang, you will feel light and your mind will become very peaceful. The energy flow in your body is very closely and intricately interconnected with your mind. The state of your Ki exists in a symbiotic relationship with your state of mind. Your state of mind has great influence over the state of your Ki, and vice versa.

When we are in a wholesome wave, we cannot hold any negative thoughts or emotions. The world of *α* wave, the world of the inner consciousness, is a world of absolute positivity, which any negative thoughts or emotions are unable to enter. Ordinary people rarely get into such a state except during their sleeping period. Keeping *α* wave when you are fully conscious, thereby not losing your inner peace and security, is the primary goal of Brain Respiration.

# C. *The Psychology of the Amygdala*

Man is generally defined either as a rational animal or as an emotional animal. Which exerts a more powerful influence on controlling human behavior, reason or emotion? Reason is the source of self-pride that man holds about his own species and the ground for his presumptuous position of the 'lord of all creation'. However, what drives man to commit certain behavior is emotions, rather than reason. We can see it very clearly when rational judgement enters into conflict with impulsive emotion..... and loses!

In many cases, emotions make fun of reason beyond the reach of our will and get their own way in everything like an arrogant tyrant. These emotions comprise the major factors which make our lives troublesome. Most people live as a slave to their emotions. These people can neither love nor trust themselves. Those who don't live as master of their own emotions will hang onto another's smiles and lose the right to be master of their own life.

How can we then control our emotions? First, through observing and contemplating the causes of our emotions, intuitively grasping them and pulling out their roots from our mind. And then we should receive the energy from the universe so that we may have enough power not to be shaken by our emotions.

If we carefully watch where our emotions come from, we can find that many of our present emotions are rooted in some experiences of the past. In fact, our brain remembers the emotions we once experienced and repeatedly plays them back. The amygdala is the part of the brain that remembers our emotions. In the amygdala, all the emotions are inscribed which have visited our life. It is absurdly difficult to erase the emotional marks once they are recorded in the amygdala.

This is why it is so hard to recover from the trauma that happened in childhood. Let us assume that you are terribly uncomfortable if you have to sing a song in front of other people. It may have nothing to do with how well you can sing. In fact, you may sing a song very well if no one is around you. You may have had the upsetting experience of being mocked by somebody about your singing. From then on, you hate singing in front of people, because the emotion of shame recorded in the amygdala manipulates your consciousness and holds back your spontaneity.

Once such a negative emotion is registered in the amygdala, whenever we are forced to face a similar situation, our brain system starts working to repeat the negative emotion.

The amygdala is like a cassette tape. In the tape, positive or negative emotions may equally be recorded. Especially as regards negative emotions, once something painful is recorded in the amygdala, it reappears repeatedly in the mind every time we are confronted with a similar situation. To be free from the prison of our emotions we need to release and erase the negative emotions stored in the amygdala. If we keep the memories, we confine our mind to the dark prison of the memories. Of course, erasing negative memories cannot be done overnight. To begin with, we have to realize that our emotions are not our true self, but negative memories inscribed in our brain.

Each of us has two kinds of self, a self and Self. The original amygdala, non-contaminated by any emotions, has a memory of the true love given from the source of life. A pure love as the essence of the cosmos is stored in the amygdala from our birth. The pure love inscribed in the amygdala is our true nature ; that is our true self. The false self is nothing but a collection of the emotions from all the experiences of our life. In a sense, life is a process of making a solid shell of the false self by covering up the true self with layers of emotion.

Unfortunately, many people look upon this false self as their true self. They do not realize that their true self is hidden and covered up by something else. This is why some people do not like themselves : they have never seen their Self, the most amazing beauty. In order to uncover the false self and see the true one, we should admit that our inner conflicts have origin in the past emotional scars, and that such emotions are not our true Self, but only a shadow of life.

A person who can look with calm reflection at the falsehood of his/her emotions will control them instead of being led by them. The story below reveals to us the falsity of our emotions.

Two persons, Andy and Bill, run a business together. They are very close friends. Andy hears from a business acquaintance that Bill cheated him by hoarding money secretly. Andy who keeps a deep trust in his friend scoffs at his remarks and doesn't believe them. But he doesn't feel at ease. One day Bill's brother says to Andy that Bill cheated Andy and that Bill privately prepared another business of his own. At this time, Andy's trust is shaken. The feeling of being betrayed by a person he trusted puts Andy into madness. Not making sure if what he was told is true, Andy takes the indirect information as fact as soon as it is put into his brain. The information greatly affects his psychology. Even if it turns out to be false, he can't easily forget the hurt he felt.

This is the way our emotions are formed and deformed by information fed into our brain. Our brain manufactures an immediate emotional reaction according to the information it receives. It does not matter whether the information is true or not. We have to keep sharp eyes on every bit of information coming into our brain to prevent false emotions from playing a trick on us.

When a certain emotion arises in the mind, most of us don't watch the emotion itself, but instead, focus our attention on the person who brought it to us. For example, if we are very angry, we turn all our attention aggressively toward the person who annoyed us. We should shift the focus from other people to ourselves. This enables us to analyze our emotions and then conquer them.

If a person traces back on the emotional circuit, one will find one's own mind-set located at the beginning of the circuit. We realize that emotional reactions come out because we have antibodies called a 'mind-set' inside us.

Let's take an example. You happen to read the diary of your roommate while you clean your room. You find he has written a lot of complaints about you in his diary. As soon as you read his writings concerning you, you become very offended. You may bitterly resent your roommate. Why do you feel offended merely for the reason that your roommate has some silent complaints about you? It is because the mind-set contained in your mind says that you should always be well spoken of by others. But how is it possible in this world where even a saint can hardly escape from quarrels and struggles? As long as you don't rid yourself of the wrong mind-set, you will continually confront such provocative situations.

We can be set free from the rule of our emotions only when we see through our mind-sets which produce them. If one sees the mind-set is the root of one's emotions, it means one's level of consciousness has been raised.

Although we have such a high level of consciousness that we 'know' how to resolve the emotional problems, the lack of energy in the heart may disable us from doing what we know.

For instance, a rich man doesn't care whether people laugh at his shabby clothes or not, while a poor man feels deeply hurt by the ridicule of others. A strong man is confident regardless of his appearance. People generally think that such strength is derived from wealth or fame. Real strength comes from the rich energy inside us. We have to get strengthened by receiving the celestial energy. Weak people think emotions are too high a mountain to climb, while strong people regard emotions as small rocks which they have only to watch out for in walking.

It is necessary to raise the level of consciousness and the level of energy at the same time. We fall into a trap of emotions if we lack energy even after reforming the emotional circuit into ideal form. What is the use of digging a ditch when no water is drawn into it? On the other hand, there is no use having plenty of energy if the consciousness stays trapped in a low level of reactive emotions. We can obtain the insight to see through the causes of our emotions and control them by receiving cosmic energy through Brain Respiration.

# D. Beyond the Limitation of the Human Body

It seems part of our human nature that we possess an unsatiable desire to challenge the unknown world. We have already set out to explore the vast space beyond the Earth. Our exploration of these mysterious areas is continuing at this moment. The exploration of the world of human consciousness is that same kind of most attractive subject waiting to be discovered. To challenge the limits of human consciousness is one of the purposes which we deeply pursue through Brain Respiration.

When we become deeply absorbed in Brain Respiration, we may have the feeling that all our organs are connected into a whole unity. We will see our body in silent contemplation. Then, we will enter the mysterious world of our body. We have two kinds of nerves and muscles; one is consciously controllable and the other is not. If we go deep into the inside of our body step by step, we come to attain the state where we can control the uncontrollable nerves and muscles. For example, we can manage the autonomic nerve system which controls the heart beating.

In general, our mind stays in the outer consciousness, which is only a tip of the giant iceberg of human consciousness. If you reach only the outer consciousness, you can have no idea of the inner world. Brain Respiration is a gate which allows easy and fruitful expedition into the inner consciousness.

If you keep practicing Brain Respiration, you can feel the connection between every part of your body and the brain. Every isolated part kept within its own section starts to open widely. Thus, you might hear your heart beating like a loud drum, or the sound of your blood stream resonating within like a waterfall. Your body may vibrate according to the sounds. These phenomena often make people confused. However, it is a powerful sign that the third brain is ready to work. You will feel that there is another world, another consciousness living outside of your individual brain. You will perceive that the cosmos has its own brain connected with human brains on the spiritual level, where you can use the universal information stored in the cosmic brain. Most of us are limited in our own small brain and feel very uneasy. When we feel the connection between our brain and the cosmic mind, we can go beyond the limitation of our physical body into the boundless realm of absolute peace and freedom.

"Awakening," or "Enlightenment" means nothing but the unification of human consciousness and the cosmic mind. It is a state of beholding the true nature of yourself. Only when you accomplish this unification, can you know who you are and why you exist.

Nowadays people are referring to MQ quite often (see Preface), but unless you experience the ultimate oneness with the cosmic consciousness, it is not possible to understand the true meaning of MQ, let alone to develop your MQ.

4

# 4. The Effects of Brain Respiration

# A. The Effects of Brain Respiration

Brain Respiration is a brain exercise which vibrates, extends, and contracts all the brain cells by Ki movements. This exercise brings fresh vitality into the brain. By doing this, it prevents aging of the brain cells and serves to correct the distorted parts of the brain. In this way, you can keep your brain healthy and your mind peaceful.

The most powerful effects of Brain Respiration come through supplying enough oxygen to the brain by the effective circulation of Ki and blood. Once your energy and blood circulation are fully activated, a lot of oxygen is delivered to the brain. Simply by creating enough oxygen, we can cure a lot of illnesses. In fact, all of our sicknesses are initiated by the irregular and poor circulation of Ki and blood.

It is stress-related difficulties which create trouble with circulation. As we often notice, modern people's upper chests are distinctively constricted because they are normally overstressed in the midst of an extremely competitive society. Continuous exposure to too much stress and ceaseless care and anxiety makes your breath shallow. The shallow breath and the small amount of air taken in make your chest inactive and constricted. Then, such a constriction produces more circulation problems and eventually causes constriction of the brain. Brain Respiration is an exercise to return the constricted brain to normal health. Therefore, the Brain Respiration exercises serve to resolve the emotional difficulties caused by the brain's constriction.

However, the most important effect of Brain Respiration is not simply therapeutic. Brain Respiration has a preventive effect for various kinds of mental or cerebral diseases. By practicing Brain Respiration, you can transform your brain into a stress-resistant brain. In fact, under the same circumstances, some people will be stressed, but others won't be. This shows that susceptibility to stress can differ according to the physical or mental conditions peculiar to each individual. Each of us has our own frame of perception, and, if things do not go well with our way of looking at life, we say that it is stressful. In short, stress has more to do with our perspective or inner responsive system to the situation, than outer circumstances.

Once you reach a state of deep meditation through Brain Respiration, your consciousness goes up to the height where you can see your mental structure. At that height of consciousness, it is possible to remove your own mind-sets just by seeing them. And then you can have a positive outlook on everything, change your personality, and enjoy better relationships with others.

The blockage of energy in the brain causes the brain cells to age quickly because your brain does not get the nutrition and energy required to keep it young and lively. This is the beginning of many various brain diseases. Nobody will dispute the fact that one of the most serious diseases of the brain is dementia. In order to prevent this fatal disease, doctors recommend that you actively use your brain. Again, Brain Respiration is a wonderful brain exercise for preventing all the brain diseases including dementia.

During these stressful times, many people are experiencing ill health, yet uncover no physical problem through a medical exam. In the modern medical field, such a case is considered to be "neurotic." Almost 80% of the patients in our modern hospitals seem to be suffering from diseases whose causes have not yet been discovered. However, seen from the viewpoint of the laws of energy, it is clear why people feel such discomfort ; the energy flow in their bodies is reversed. Once your body regain the proper balance between fire and water energy, Su Song Wha Gang, then, all the symptoms you have been suffering from will disappear naturally. You will feel light and fresh.

Brain Respiration is also very effective for overweight people. Ki as the bio-energy, has the power of rejuvenating. By practicing it, you can have an ideal weight ; if you are obese, you could become slim, and vice versa. As we see, the western style of diet seems to be too rich to maintain a human's proper weight. I believe that Brain Respiration could be one of the most natural ways to control the Weight problems.

These days many people are aware of the limitation of the left brain dominated personality, and have great interest in developing their right brain in order to have a balance between the two halves of the brain. Brain Respiration is strongly effective in activating the right brain. By developing the right half of your brain, you can increase creativity and EQ.

Brain Respiration, by which we control the flow of energy, is training for using the power of the mind consciously. Through Brain Respiration, we come to believe that infinite divinity exists in ourselves and that all things around us are just the images projected by our minds. By realizing this, we can obtain the ability to form new values in an empty space where all the existing ideas have been swept away. Through Brain Respiration, we can confirm the possibility of things which we think belong to the world of the impossible. We can make practical use of the hitherto unexplored functions of our body and brain.

Further, in the advanced levels of Brain Respiration, you can experience your consciousness becoming one with the cosmic mind. At this level, you can go beyond your physical body. In such unity with the universe, you will realize what is truly the vital essence of life and the true nature of the universe. Then, your life will be lived from its clear vision of the future. In the advanced level of Brain Respiration, MQ, which is the ultimate index of human development, will dramatically improve by decoding the secrets of the fourth dimensional cosmic consciousness.

# 5. Warming-up for Brain Respiration

Before you start Brain Respiration,
you need to make yourself fully relaxed.
Let's do some exercises to make your body and
mind ready for Brain Respiration.

# A. Stretching and Relaxing Exercises for Brain Respiration

In order to practice Brain Respiration, your mind and body need to be relaxed. The following stretching will help you to be relaxed and ready for Brain Respiration.

When you do the following stretching exercise, you must totally focus on the part of your body which you are stretching. For example, if you do a neck exercise, concentrate on your neck and feel that part. Have a kind of conversation with your body. Do it slowly, in your own rhythm.

It would be better if you can do the exercise together with your breathing. At the beginning, focus on your pose first. Once you get used to the pose, pay attention to your breathing. You inhale when you start to take a pose, and then exhale when you return to the original position.

Now, let's begin with neck exercise and shoulder exercise. Neck and shoulders stiffen first when we suffer from stress and tension. When our neck and shoulders are stiff, our head feels very heavy. The blocked circulation of blood and energy due to the stiffness around these areas prevents the smooth provision of fresh oxygen and energy to the brain cells. Just by lightly moving our neck and shoulders we can feel the muscles relax and our head is refreshed. In doing neck exercise, move your neck gently. It is a weak joint.

# N ECK EXERCISE

1) Put your hands on your waist, straighten your spine and relax your shoulders. Put your head down toward your chest, as far as you can. Feel the stretch in the back side of your neck. Inhale when your head goes forward, and exhale when it returns to the original position.

2) Slowly put your head backward. Inhale when your head goes backward, and exhale when it returns to the original position. Repeat this exercise a few times.

3) Turn your head to the left as far as you can.

4) Then, turn your head to the right. Inhale when you turn your head, and exhale when it returns to the original position. Repeat this exercise a couple of times.

5) Keep your face straight and let your left ear touch the left shoulder.

6) Then, touch the right ear to the right shoulder, again inhaling whenever you start to take a pose, and exhaling when you finish it.

7) Make a circle with your head a couple of times, first clockwise;

8) then, counter-clockwise.

## S HOULDER EXERCISE

Pull up your shoulders, until they can almost touch your ears, inhaling when you raise the shoulders, and exhaling when you lower them. Do this several times, until your shoulders are completely relaxed.

Lightly clasp your shoulders with your hands and make a circle with your elbows. When you rotate your arm, you

should feel that your shoulders are rotating together. Make a circle forward a few times and then circle backward a few times.

# CHEST EXERCISE

Stretch your arms forward and place your palms together. Widely spread out your arms on both sides and go backwards as far as you can, in order to open up your chest area. Inhale when you extend your arms, and exhale returning to the original position. Repeat this exercise with the proper breathing several times.

An important meridian is located in the middle of our chest. It is a major channel for the flow of "Ki" and is called "Immack" in Korean. The state of "Immack" tends to be directly influenced by our emotions. The chest

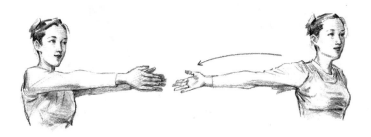

meridian is easily blocked by negative emotions in the chest. On the whole, modern people under too much stress have "Immack" seriously blocked. The blockage at the chest meridian hinders deep breathing and causes headaches. The Chest Exercise helps you particularly with deep breathing.

With your fingertips, gently tap the top of your head. Then, tap all over the head in the same way, until you feel fresh and revitalized.

## TAPPING YOUR HEAD AND NECK

Continue to tap your forehead, temple, around your eyes, cheekbone, cheek, under the ear, and your jaw. Also, tap all around your mouth, to stimulate your gums.

With your palms, pat the backside of your neck. Sometimes you may feel the sensation created by this exercise traveling all the way down to your feet.

# P ATTING YOUR WHOLE BODY

Each meridian has its own direction of circulation. Therefore, when we do the patting exercise over our whole body, we do this according to the meridian flows. Do this exercise when you get up in the morning, since it is so invigorating. It will open up any blockages which have created circulation problems in your body.

1) Raise your left arm forward, palm down with your right hand, pat your left shoulder down to the back of your hand. Turn the palm up and gradually pat back up the in-

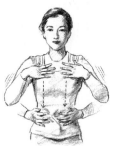

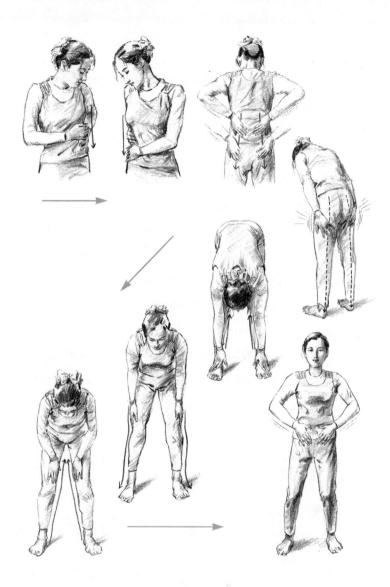

side arm to shoulder.

2) Change your arms; right hand is forward, palm down. Start patting with your left hand from your right shoulder, continuing as in number one.

3) Now, pat all around your chest with both your palms. Go to the side and pat all over the upper torso, your rib bones, stomach, and side. Feel your internal organs. If there is any pain, such a spot needs more care and attention. This area will improve with practice everyday.

4) Go to the lower back and pat all over. This stimulates your kidneys. Then go to the buttocks.

5) Pat all the way down your back legs to your ankle. Then come up along the front side of the legs.

6) Pat around your hip joint in the groin area, and once again, come down along the side of the legs. Starting at the ankle, come up again along the inside of legs.

7) Finally, pat your abdomen. When you pat your Dahn-jon, place your feet apart about shoulder width and slightly bend your knees.

# STIMULATING THE SOLES OF YOUR FEET

You can do this pose either sitting on the floor, or in a chair. First, put your left foot on your right thigh. With both your thumbs, press the sole of your foot all over, thoroughly. If you feel any pain, press that area some more. Then, press along the inside area of your leg, moving up to the thigh. Hold your foot with your left hand, make a fist with your right hand and hit your sole thoroughly. Pay more attention to the middle point of your sole, where there is a slight curve. Strike this point a little bit longer.

Reverse the pose and do the same exercise.

As all the meridians of your body gather at your feet, stimulating your feet also effectively stimulates your brain.

# B. Feeling the Sensation of "Ki" Energy

# FEELING IT BETWEEN THE HANDS

As we described in the previous chapter, Brain Respiration is a brain exercise of Ki movement. In order to do Brain Respiration, first of all, you have to develop your 6th sense, the feeling of your invisible bio-energy. As every living thing depends on this vitality from the universe, living beings, including human beings, can feel the energy.

The first thing you need to do to develop your 6th sense is to accept the existence of energy. Ki, bio-energy, is not visible, so it is hard to sense it with our five basic senses-smell, sound, sight, touch, and taste. We need to discover the 6th sense for this energy flow to be experienced in our body. The 6th sense is one of our innate per-

ceptions, which has been lost due to our predisposition to deny the world of the unseen.

If you are clinging to outer consciousness, such as the five basic senses or to the emotions, you cannot enter the world of Ki. Only when you arrive in the inner world through a concentrated mind, will your 6th sense be rediscovered. We call this part of the exercise, "Ji Gam Suryn," which implies detaching from the outer consciousness and going into the inner consciousness. Literally, Ji Gam means to stop being distracted by the impressions of the five senses and the emotions.

Now, allow yourself to feel your own Ki through

your hands.

Make yourself comfortable. You can sit either on the floor or on a chair. Gently rock your upper torso and hips back and forth, right and left, in order to center yourself. Be sure that your spine is straight. With your palms upward, gently put your hands on your knee. Close your eyes. Relax yourself, and do not hold any tension in your body. Check to see what part of your body might still be tense. The neck and shoulders are often common spots where people easily hold their tension. Make sure that these areas are fully relaxed. Take a deep breath, and with the exhalation, send all the stagnated energy out of your body. You may make a sound when you exhale.

Slowly lift your hands from the knees to the chest and form a prayer position. Your whole attention is on your hands. Keep your eyes closed and try to see your hands in front of your chest with your mind. Imagine the shape of your hands. Sense the feelings in your hands. Do not miss any subtle sensation of your hands. Totally focus on your hands.

In your hands, there is a blood stream from the heart. If

you stay focused, you can sense the warm heat in your hands. Feel the warmth of your own body temperature. Try to listen to your heart beat through that stream in your hands. Then, feel the pulsation of the blood vessels in your hands, according to your heart beat. Concentrate your awareness on the fingertips and keep sensing the pulsation of your hands. Call to your hands silently, without speaking out loud: "Hands, hands, hands···" And, consciously notice if there is any other sensation in your hands.

Now, slowly take your hands apart from each other, leaving a space of about two inches between them. You must never get tense. Make sure that your shoulders are relaxed. Feel as if both your hands are hanging in the air. Between your hands, a strong energy field is forming. Seeing your hands with your mind, imagine the energy between your palms. It may look like light or a cloud. The energy between your hands is full and shining. Also, it flows like a cloud.

Now, make the space between your hands wider and narrower. Attune your mind to the feeling found in your hands. You may feel some electric sensation between your hands. Such a sensation could vary—it could be very subtle or quite strong.

You may feel that there is some soft jello between your hands. It is like the feeling you have when you put your hands under water to play with the liquid movement against the fingers and palms. It may feel like the touch of a gentle breeze. It is hard to describe this sensation, as you, yourself, have to feel the energy.

Also, you might feel some magnetic power between your hands, as if each side of your palms becomes like a magnetic pole. It may feel like there is a magnetic attraction between your hands. Do not miss any sensation; just focus on any feeling that arises. At the beginning, it might feel quite subtle and weak, but once you focus on the energy, it will become stronger and clearer.

If the sensation of the energy between your hands becomes clear, enlarge your hand movements. Move your hands according to the flow of energy and enjoy the feelings of this life-giving energy.

# ERECTING A PILLAR OF ENERGY ON YOUR PALMS

Now, let's try to feel the energy in a different way. Face your palms up at the level of your abdomen. Then slowly raise one hand and lower the other. Reverse the movement. Continue to change the position of your hands.

Focus on your hands and move very slowly. Soon you will feel some tingling sensation in your fingertips and some weight in the middle of your palms, as if there is a pillar of energy from the palms to the sky. According to your hands' movement, the pillar seems to be extended (down) or contracted (up).

At first, you will be moving your hands consciously. But, soon you will feel that your hands are moving by themselves, without your own effort.

# D RAWING CIRCLES WITH YOUR HANDS

This time, put your palms facing each other and rotate your hands as if drawing circles. Rotate one hand forward and the other backward. And then reverse the direction of each hand. Imagine that you are holding a ball in

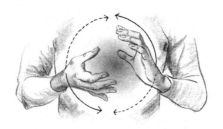

your hands and are playing with it. If you concentrate well, you can actually feel the energy gathering into a lump with elasticity like a ball between your hands. Again, you may have either an electric sensation or a magnetic attraction between your hands. Everybody has a different sensation, so try to find your own feelings, totally concentrating on yourself.

# ENDING THE EXERCISE

After you do this exercise for 10 minutes, make a prayer position. Then, focus your consciousness onto your Dahnjon. Continually call your Dahnjon in your mind. When you call your Dahnjon, the energy in your hands goes into your body—through your arm, chest, and finally reaches into the Dahnjon. In this way, energy is accumulated in your Dahnjon.

Now, open your eyes, while rubbing your palms fast. Once you feel the warmth in your palms, put your hands over your open eyes, and send the warm vitality into your eyeballs. Rotate your eyeballs upward, downward, then left and right. Make a circle with your eyeball. Again, while

rubbing your hands, massage your face and neck with your warm hands.

You are just recovering the 6th sense, which has been forgotten for a long time. Even if you may not feel so clear about these sensations, do not be discouraged. If you keep practicing the exercises, the 6th sense will come. This 6th sense is not something to learn, it is something that you re-discover. Just relax your mind and body, and concentrate on the sensation of Ki. The only thing that you need to do is to open your mind wide to cosmic energy.

## 6. Brain Respiration Exercises

# A. Beginner's Level of Exercise

Please take a seat and make yourself comfortable. You can either sit on a chair or sit on the floor. Make sure that your spine is straight and there is no tension in your neck and shoulders. It is important to make yourself fully relaxed before you start Brain Respiration exercises. As a way to be relaxed, you could do some stretching exercises introduced briefly in the previous chapter. Then, you do the "Jigam" exercise—the exercise that guides you into feeling an electric sensation between your hands— for a while. Jigam exercise is a first step for Brain Respiration, which increases your ability to concentrate.

Brain Respiration is an exercise based on your imagination. Therefore, you should place no limitation on using your imagination. The beginner needs to start with about 20 to 30 minutes for one practice. Once you get used to doing that, 5 to 10 minutes of exercise will be enough. When you are in Brain Respiration, you are in a deep meditative state. Carefully watch all the changes happening in your body. Twice a day practice of these exercises would be ideal, just after arising in the morning and, again before going to bed.

# E XERCISE 1
## WATCHING AND FEELING YOUR BRAIN

Make yourself comfortable. If you sit on a chair, put both your hands on your thighs. Or, sit on the floor in the half lotus pose and wrap your knees with your hands.

Take three deep breaths: inhale and exhale, inhale and exhale, and inhale and exhale. Breathing slowly, exhale all the tension out of your whole body, through the fingertips and the toes. Watch your Dahnjon with your mind's eyes for a while.

Now focus on your brain. Watch your brain through your mind and relax each part of your brain by sending

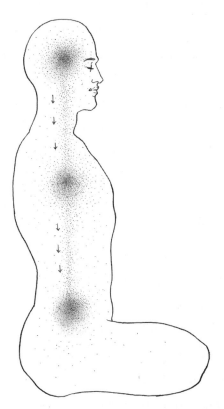

Before practising Brain Respiration whatever level of exercise you do, you should bring your energy down to Dahnjon by moving consciousness to that area. Taking a comfortable position with your eyes closed, first think of the top of the head and then shift concentration from it through the chest, to Dahnjon. If you speak out each of those three parts-the top of the head, the chest, the Dahnjon, it will help to concentrate. After that, breathe in and out three times.

Ki. See the brain through your mind, imagining that you see things through your 6th sense. With the power of your imagination, you are taking a journey into the brain.

Seeing through your mind, call to each part of your brain sincerely, as if you are calling your dear lover. Wherever your mind goes, energy follows. It is a primary principle of the universe. Cerebrum, cerebellum, cerebrum, cerebellum··· Call each part of your brain with loving and care. It will be of great help to be focused. Then listen carefully to how your brain responds to you. There must be an answering to your call. In this way, you have a conversation with your brain.

Feel first the hard surface of the skull. Then, go inside of your brain where each part of your brain, such as the cerebrum, the cerebellum, the midbrain, and the interbrain come together; a place where you can overview each of them.

Next, we will focus on each one of these parts of the brain more closely. Focus your consciousness on the cerebrum, the largest part of your brain. Calling, cerebrum,

cerebrum, cerebrum···.

There are bridges between your right and left brain. In order to have a healthy and balanced brain function, these bridges must be strong and well connected with each other. However, in our left brain dominated society, the bridges between the right and left brain are almost disconnected. Move your focus on the right and then on the left continually, while you imagine that you are strengthening the bridges between the two.

Let's pay more attention to our right side of the brain. Our right side of the brain may look like a house abandoned long ago. Send your love and care to the right side of the brain, where your creativity can endlessly be produced.

Now, let's focus on the cortex of the cerebrum. Front and back, up and down, and both sides. Look all over the cerebrum. You may want to send more care to the front part, on the forehead, which is where the most energetic brain activities happen.

In the deeper parts of the cerebrum, is the amygdala which controls human emotions. This first time, you may

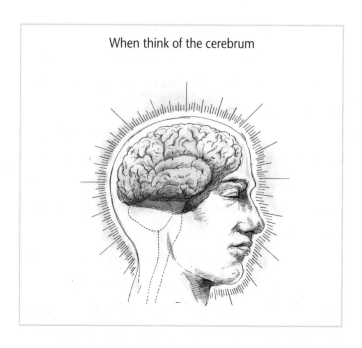

When think of the cerebrum

not find the location of the amygdala. However, with more practice, you can feel it. Keep watching your cerebrum and call the amygdala. Amygdala, amygdala, amygdala···.

Now, let's take a look at the cerebellum. The cerebellum is smaller than the cerebrum and is located under the cerebrum. Call to the cerebellum, cerebellum, cerebellum···.

The interbrain is hidden between the cerebrum and the

cerebellum. Now send your love and appreciation to this part of the brain, which greatly enhances the feeling of aliveliness in our body. Interbrain, interbrain, interbrain···.

You should not miss the hypophysis, even though it is quite small. Hypophysis is the source of an internal hormone. Imagine the flow of the hormone produced from this part of your brain. Hypophysis, hypophysis, hypophysis···.

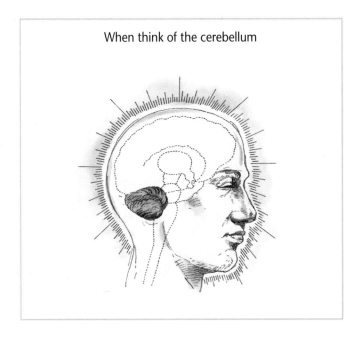

When think of the cerebellum

Underneath the hypophysis, there is the midbrain. Midbrain, midbrain, midbrain···.

Let's go to the bulb at the back side of your neck. If there is any damage to the bulb, your life is threatened. Also, send positive energy to the bulb.

For the last, look at your spinal cord. The spinal cord looks like a long cylinder. Spinal cord, spinal cord, spinal cord···.

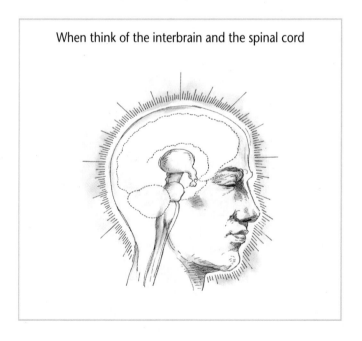

When think of the interbrain and the spinal cord

Now, your whole brain is totally relaxed. Only when your brain is fully relaxed, can your consciousness be released from the brain. Once your consciousness is detached from the brain, look at the brain for 20 seconds. Look around your brain in the following sequence:cerebrum→the left side of your brain→the right side of your brain→cortex of the cerebrum→amygdala→cerebrum→cerebellum→ interbrain→hypophysis→midbrain→bulb→spinal cord. Repeat this exercise several times.

After viewing your whole brain, take three deep breaths. When you exhale, imagine that the used energy in your brain is going out of your body. Even though I use the term imagination, such phenomena is really happening at the energy level. Until your 6th sense is fully activated, use your imagination for initiative. Rub your hands fast. Then with the warm heat in your palms, massage your face and your head.

When you look at each part of your brain, imagine that warm sunshine is illuminating the focused spot. Just as sunshine has the power to melt ice, any tension in your brain will readily dissolve. Just as plants will grow from the sun's energy, your brain cells are creating vitality from the sun.

Seeing and naming each part of your brain is like contacting an organic living being. You can feel the breathing of each brain cell. You can even hear the blood stream in your brain vessels.

If somebody calls your name softly, to give you attention, it always feels so pleasant and caring. Such a warm feeling is nourishing not only for humans, but every creation in the universe wants love and attention. Your body is not an exception. With the gentle calling of each name, your own brain cells are moved, vibrated and awakened. If you can concentrate without disturbing your five senses, you will feel the joy of your brain deeply within your heart.

# EXERCISE 2    BREATHING THROUGH THE MAJOR ACUPRESSURE POINTS IN YOUR HEAD.

Just as the vital energy fluctuates in the vast ocean of universal life, the same energy flows through our body. In our body, there is a road for this energy flow. Throughout each road, there are many intersections

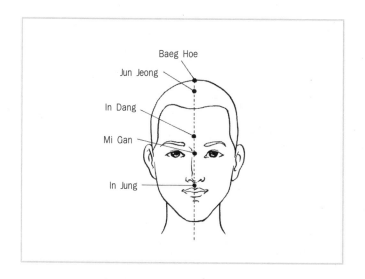

Baeg Hoe
Jun Jeong
In Dang
Mi Gan
In Jung

like stations, where the energy from the universe comes and goes. We call theses roads meridians, and the intersections, acupressure points.

Now, I will explain how you can breath through those acupressure points in your head. For this exercise, you have to know the major acupressure points in your head.

**Baeg Hoe :** Located at the top of the head. It means that a hundred meridians meet each other at this point. When you were a baby, this point was soft. Once you recover the 6th sense through our exercises, you will receive celestial

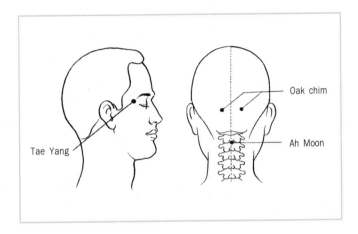

Tae Yang

Oak chim

Ah Moon

energy through this point. Thus, we call this acupressure point the great gate toward Heaven.

**Jun Jeong :** Located 2 inches forward of Baeg Hoe. Like Baeg Hoe, this point is also an energy receiving one, so it is called the small gate to Heaven. The difference is, that through Baeg Hoe you can receive any kind of energy. Through Jun Jeong, you can only receive highly purified energy.

**In Dang :** Located between your eyebrows. Once this acupressure point is opened and functional, you could have clairvoyant power to see through all manner of things··· It is called "the eye of Heaven", or what might also be referred to as, "The Third Eye".

**Mi Gan** : Located between the eyes.

**Tae Yang** : Located at each temple.

**In Jung** : Located at the middle point, between the nose and upper lip.

**Ah Moon** : Located on the border line between your neck and the bottom of your skull. If this point is blocked, people often have difficulties speaking.

**Oak Chim** : Located 1 inch apart from the projecting spot, which is in the lower part of the middle line at the back of your head.

Slowly move your consciousness in the following progression. When you focus on each acupressure point, call the name of each point silently within the mind. Or say it out loud. When you pronounce the name of each location, make the sound long and slow with your breathing.

Baeg Hoe~, Jun Jeong~, In Dang~, Mi Gan~,
In Jung~, Ah Moon~, Oak Chim~, Baeg Hoe~,
Jun Jeong~, and so on.

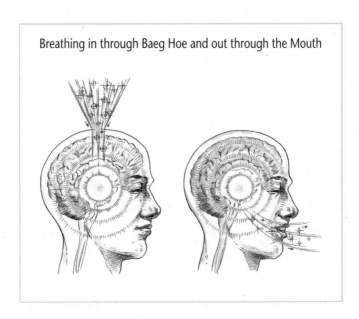

Breathing in through Baeg Hoe and out through the Mouth

Imagine that when you call the name of each acupressure point, a big hole opens up at each point. Because of all kinds of stress, modern human's acupressure points are often blocked. Through the concentration on each acupressure point, you can open up each energy point in your head.

Now, let's take a breath with a feeling focused on each acupressure point. When inhaling, focus your consciousness on Baeg Hoe. Imagine that the cosmic vitality enters into Baeg Hoe. Then, exhale through your mouth with the sound, "Hu—"

Do the same breathing exercise with the rest of the acupressure points:In Dang, Mi Gan, Tae Yang, In Jung, Ah Moon, Oak Chim. If you do this exercise with pure concentration, you will feel that the pressure points are opening up and are receiving fresh vitality through the points. After all this, you should now feel so light and fresh in your head!

Particularly, Baeg Hoe is a most important point for preventing dementia and amnesia. Keep this pressure point opened up, as it is so crucial for having a healthy brain.

# EXERCISE 3
## LAUGHING EXERCISE

Now, Let's do a more interesting Brain Respiration Exercise.

Find a small mirror and observe your face for a while. Look very carefully at your face. People say that one's face is the reflection of his/her mind. How about your own face? What kind of reflection appears? Is your face shining or

Laughing Exercise : When you frown, you find your brain and chest constricted and uneasy. When you laugh, they become relaxed and peaceful.

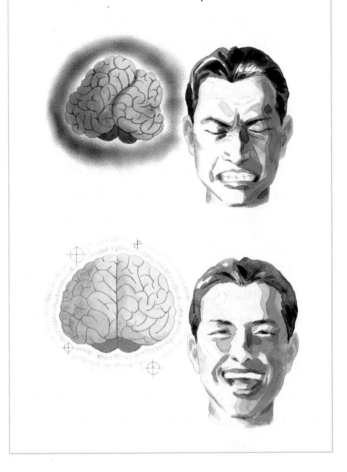

gloomy? Is it tensed, or relaxed? Joyful or irritated? Or, is it more or less blank?

Smile at yourself in the mirror. Watch your smile. Does your smile look natural and comfortable, or not? Is your facial expression too hard because of tension to express a big smile? If you feel too uneasy to smile a big smile, you may have to check your mind. If your mind also gets hard like your face, explore the possibility that your hardened face symbolizes your closed mind.

Now, relax your shoulders and close your eyes. Then smile gently. Can you feel that your face and brain become relaxed with your smiling? Soon you will feel the same comfort in your heart, as there is an energy line that connects your heart to your brain. Now then, let's make a frowning face. As soon as you make your face distorted, the energy center in your heart is blocked and your brain gets tense. This makes sense when you consider that your smiling and laughing are so positively affective to your brain. Repeat the above exercise several times; first, smiling and, then, making a frowning face. This exercise is excellent stimulation for the brain.

This time, when you make a smile, watch carefully the changes that happen in your body. Smile calmly and you can feel your facial muscles relaxed and the tension around your chest released. Now, make a big smile and concentrate on your brain. See if you have the sensation that your skull and brain cells are comfortably relaxed. A person with a keen sense of feeling "Ki" may experience pure, fresh energy coming into the brain.

If you smile while concentrating on your brain, you can truly feel the unity between your heart and brain. Further, feel the heart center start to open widely with the most peaceful and pure energy, which then emanates into your whole body. This energy from the heart has a purifying power.

With the most joyful face, tell yourself: "I am so happy and comfortable." Your smile will bring happiness from your heart.

Of course, you are not smiling because you are feeling especially joyful right now. You simply smile without any reason. However, you will find that your mind gets brighter, once you smile. As you smile, you might feel any anxiety or impatience disappear, or something which has held you tightly, fade away.

A lot of smiling or laughing is the best exercise for the brain. It is the most effective way to supply oxygen to the brain. Once you start to smile and laugh, there is joy coming from your heart. Such joyfulness may not come from

any particular source. It was, and is there, inside of us from the beginning. However, it was blocked with various stressful emotions and thoughts. Once the blockage is cleared, this wellspring of joy is free to flow.

The interaction between our inside self and outside self is very interesting. As you know, smiling is an expression of the joyfulness of your mind. We take it for granted that whenever we feel happy, we smile and laugh. However, instead of passively responding to your emotions, consciously change your mood to a more positive one. Your emotions are not something only created from your inside. You, by yourself, can create your own emotions. This is why the human being is the lord of all the creatures. If you know this fact really well, you will not be led by your emotions, but will lead and create your own mood.

Therefore, if you feeling sad or unhappy, instead of sitting in a dark room alone and falling into melancholic feelings, make a big smile and laugh. Even if it is an artificial laughing, it still provides positive power to your mind. Just as your inside affects your appearance, your outer expression affects your inside. If your mind is gloomy and dark, make some smiles to make it bright and light again.

Try to smile as frequently as possible even on purpose. When you smile, the feeling accompanying your smile, joy, is recorded in your brain. Think of joy in the act of smiling brightly and this pleasant emotion is then stored in your brain. At first, you may have to put some efforts into smiling. If you make such efforts at least five times, as soon as you press the key of smile, joy is automatically played on the piano of your heart. Once it becomes a habit, it does not take too long to bring out the joy from your heart.

Now, laugh intensely, shaking your body. Laugh so intensely as to feel faint. At first, make your face laugh, then your chest, your belly button, and finally your toes. When you are laughing, every energy center in your body is wide open up from the top of your brain to the bottom of your feet. You will be brimming over with energy.

A laugh is not just a laugh. Your brain experiences a transformation simply by laughing one time. Your brain has to exercise a lot for a laugh. When you laugh, joyous memories in the amygdala begin to work while you are unconscious of it.

If you will laugh so intensely as to feel faint, you will be using brain nerves and facial muscles which you do not ordinarily use. As most of our brains are usually constricted owing to much tension, not enough oxygen is supplied to our brain. Laughing is an effective way of awakening your brain and supplying abundant oxygen there. Laughing puts you into natural Brain Respiration and carries to you the same effects as bodily exercises do. It is better to laugh for five minutes than to exercise for five hours. Continuing to laugh this way, you will see your face and skeleton change. You will enjoy good health. Your life will totally change. Whenever you look in the mirror, whenever you meet other people, or when you are alone in your room, laugh to the fullest! It is what your brain wants.

# B. Intermediate Level of Brain Respiration Exercise

E
## XERCISE 1

## EXPANDING AND CONTRACTING THE BRAIN

### *Ji Gam Exercise for Warming Up*

Sitting in a comfortable pose, make your palms face each other and lift them up to chest level. Make sure that your palms are not touching each other. There should be some space—about an inch—between your hands.

Imagine that each of your palms becomes a small magnetic board. Concentrate on your hands. Now, call your hands telepathically. Hands, hands, hands···. You will soon feel an electric sensation between your hands.

Once you get the feeling, slowly take your hands apart,

your concentration remaining on your hands. Again, slowly put your hands together without them touching each other. Repeat this movement several times, very slowly.

When you move your hands apart, it is like the magnetic field created between like magnetic poles, which repel each other. When you put your hands together, it is like the magnetic field created between unlike magnetic poles, which attract each other. Once you can feel the magnetic field around your hands, you can sense the same kind of magnetic field around your brain. In fact, the human brain is a type of magnet which is interconnected with the powerful magnetic field of the universe.

### Hand movements, along with breathing

Now, try to connect the movements of your hands with your breathing. When you inhale, your hands move apart. When you exhale, your hands come together. Keep moving your hands and imagine your lungs. When your hands are apart, your lungs becomes expanded. When your hands come together, the lungs contract. When your lungs are expanded, fresh air is coming into your brain, like a cool

breeze. When your lungs are contracted, the used air is going out from your body, like the tides of the ocean. The deeper your breathing is, the more strongly the magnetic field surrounds your brain.

### Hand movements along with the brain

Now, let's connect your hand movements with your brain. Simply extend the sensation between your hands up to your brain. Imagine that your brain is your hand. You can freely move your brain, just as you do your hands. Take your left hand as your left side of the brain, and the right hand as your right side of the brain. As soon as you use your hands as the brain, your hands and the brain are interconnected immediately by sensory nerves. By moving your hands apart and bringing them together, you can pull and push your left and right brain from both sides. You will now feel the same magnetic attraction in your hands as found in your brain.

When you take your hands apart, your brain is extended, too. Imagine one big circle. The circle gets wider and wider. When you put your hands close together, your brain contracts. The big circle becomes one point.

Or, you could imagine that there is a balloon in your brain. When you take a breath, the balloon gets bigger. Exhaling, the air of the balloon goes out and the balloon gets smaller.

### The connection between the brain and the heartbeat

You have felt how your brain expands and contracts according to your breathing. Once you gain a sense of connection between your breathing and your brain, the next challenge is to connect your heart's beating with your brain's movement. Imagine the blood from the heart is rushing into your brain at each pulse. Imagine a pipe between your heart and your brain. Open up the pipe as wide as you can so the blood can easily flow into your brain. The pressure from the blood flow could feel so strong that you may even feel seriously shaken.

Through this imaginative process, you can compare the normal condition of your blood flow to the feeling of double the amount of blood rushing into your brain vitalizing each cell of your brain with more oxygen. Such nourishment from the blood will cause each cell of your brain to become refreshed and awakened, like fresh green sprouts coming up from the desert floor after a lovely spring rain.

Later, when you become adept at Brain Respiration, you can do it without initiating any hand movements. For easy concentration, at the beginner's level, you can connect hand movements with the brain. First of all, you will feel the electric sensation between your hands. Then, you will make a connection between the hand movements and the brain, then between the brain and the heart. Once you feel a complete connection between the heart and the brain, try putting your hands down and continue breathing. Place your palms up and put your hands on both your knees. Let any shoulder tension flow out through your fingertips. While practicing your deep breathing in a comfortable position, you will again feel the connection between your heart and the brain. Also, feel the connection through your heartbeat, as well as feel every part of your body interconnected to the other. Then, you can very easily enter into a meditation state in which you observe your own body.

### Ending the exercise

By taking three deep breaths, your awareness will come back to ordinary consciousness. Move your concentration to your Dahnjon and accumulate "Ki" at your Dahnjon. Take a deep breath, focusing on your Dahnjon. Inhale and exhale, inhale and exhale, inhale deeply one last time, and then bend the upper part of your body while exhaling through your mouth, making a "sss" sound between your teeth. Rub your hands and massage your face.

Once you feel the magnetic field formed around your hands through the hand movements, you can also feel that same magnetic field around your brain, too. In fact, the human brain is a magnet connected with a powerful universal magnetic field. The deeper your breathing becomes, the more your brain is completely surrounded by this magnetic field. If you fully concentrate to connect the brain and the heart's beating, you will feel that the magnetic field surrounding the brain grow clearer and stronger.

The essential intent of this exercise is to create a connection between the heart and the brain. Through Brain Respiration, you will eventually feel that your heart and brain have become one. During each breathing exercise, your brain is growing; and it is the same with the heart. Finally your expanded heart and brain become one huge shining ball of light.

Furthermore, the feeling of this connection also reaches deeply into the lower Dahnjon (the second chakra), while your whole body gets larger and smaller, according to your heart's beating. If you keep doing this kind of breathing for 30 minutes, your whole body becomes completely puri-fied. All the tiredness and used energy will disappear in the midst of the purified energy field around your body. Your body is transformed into a state of purified blissful energy.

Remember, Brain Respiration is an exercise based on the imagination. During the practice of these exercises, keep imagining that your brain is richly expanding, and also picture that the magnetic energy field is now being created around your brain.

As soon as your imagination creates such a picture, your brain immediately records that information like a comput-er programmed to save vital data. When such information is received, your brain is transformed by this energetic data.

Sounds like magic? Yes, but because the human brain nerves have a very complicated synapse system, they can deal with these large amounts of information within a few seconds.

# EXERCISE 2
## MASSAGING THE BRAIN

Sit in a comfortable pose and close your eyes. Place your hands on your knees, and while taking deep breaths, allow your body and mind to be completely relaxed. Move your concentration from your head, through your chest, to your Dahnjon and connect these three parts in one line.

Slowly lift your hands and make a prayer position at the level of your chest. Focus your consciousness on your hands. Hand, hand, hand, hand, hand···. Imagine that all of your body is disappearing, except your hands. Your hands become warm and you can feel the heart's pulsation in them.

Now, slowly move your hands apart. Once the space between your hands become chest wide, stop moving your hands. Then, feel all ten fingers as if you were playing the piano, moving your fingers. Twist your wrists. Again, place your hands together until the space between the palms is only two inches apart. Do this exercise while creating a feeling or sensation of energy.

Keep focusing on your hands by moving them apart, and then together, several times. During this process, you can accumulate a very pure and clean energy. Finally, turn your hands into the pure and clean energy itself.

Again, put your hands on your knees, and with a deep breath, focus on your brain. Once your body and mind are completely relaxed through deep and comfortable breathing, you can see into the blockages or the distorted parts of your brain. You can also begin to see the overly constricted parts or the misplaced parts of your brain cells. Just as one of your eyes could be larger than the other, your brain could possibly be crooked in the process of its formation.

Now, let's place your hands into your brain. Begin massaging it like you are playing with some rubber dough. Of course, it is your imaginative hands that are playing now, not your actual hands. Your hands will remain on your knees.

If any wrinkled part of the brain appears, make it even. If

it is bent, make it straight. If it is over constricted, gently smooth and massage it.

You can also play with your brain like a ball. Turn it into every direction—right and left, up and down, wherever you feel like you want to nurture your brain.

If you find any hardened part, gently stretch and squeeze the brain to soften it. If it is too hard to be softened, then carefully rub it in a circular movement.

Keep concentrating on your brain and massage it imaginaly. Let' s extend your brain in every direction, above and below, right and left, and then at diagonal angles. Everybody finds their favorite direction by doing this exercise. Some of you feel more comfortable when you do this along a vertical line. Others feel good when they practice this imaging along the horizontal way. Practicing this exercise can change your brain shape. Because the shape of your brain has to do with your personality, doing this brain exercise can help you to change your personality. Do you think that your face is too long? Then, extend your brain into the right side of your face, and then the left. You could change the shape of your face, as well as your personality.

Keep concentrating on your brain and touch it here and there. Massage your brain and reshape it with the energy flow.

There are many reasons why the brain may be deformed or overconstricted. Obstetricians use artificial metal instruments to pull out the head of a baby in some cases of hard labor. Such an act can easily create a brain deformity, because the baby's skull at the moment of birth is so delicate and soft. Having a baby during wartime is another example. The stress during these times might not allow adequate medical care. Thereafter, once your brain gets constricted, your mind does, too.

As you can see, it is important to have proper placement of your brain and to allow the brain cells to develop unconstricted. Any deformity creates emotional or personality problems. In many cases, people easily blame each other, even though troubles often stem from a damaged brain, and over and over, people love to blame themselves. Either approach is not an appropriate solution.

Through Brain Respiration, you can restore your brain to a healthy alignment. Of course, you can make your brain

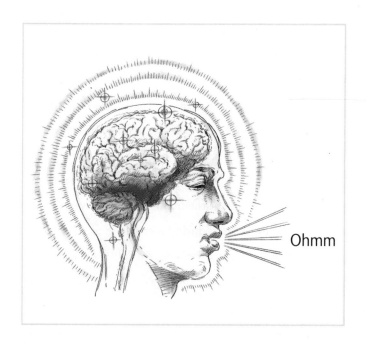

Ohmm

relaxed, that is why your brain feels so clear and re-freshed after Brain Respiration.

When you keep concentrating on Brain Respiration in a fully relaxed state of consciousness, you may hear sudden sounds, like the cracking of bones. These are sounds from your brain cells which were constricted and are now releasing. Once the previous distortion of your brain is reshaped, your body will be transformed.

# EXERCISE 3
## VIBRATING THE BRAIN WITH SOUND

The third exercise is about creating brain vibrations through vocal sound. It is an exercise using sound waves that cause the brain to vibrate in a concentrated manner and heal itself.

Energy is composed of these three elements; light, sound, and waves. Light, sound and waves are all a form of energy. Thus, this exercise is a way to revitalize your brain by sending energy through sound.

Let's start : You can sit, lie down, or stand. Any kind of pose is acceptable. Close your eyes and focus on the sound you create. See how the vibration of your vocal sound affects your brain. Ohmm....Ohmm.... The waves of your vocal sound enter the brain and vibrate each cell with circular movements. Ohmm is the sound which can vibrate the whole brain. It awakens and activates the brain.

Now, place your hands on your chest and say Ohmm. With that particular sound, if you focus fully on the vibration, you may feel as if your whole body melts into the void. At the beginning, your breathing will not last too long. But, the more you practice, the longer you can sustain your breath. Your thoughts and emotions can be stopped by creating this Ohmm sound with a concentrated mind.

You may sound Ohmm like a humming bird.

As I stated before, the sound you create is a form of energy. Each sound carries five different energies—tree, fire, soil, metal, and water. The Ohmm sound is a combination of all five elements. As first, it is your brain which vibrates the most with the Ohmm sound, but soon you can feel the whole body vibrating. As the vibration of Ohmm cleans and balances your total energy field, the daily practice of sounding Ohmm will greatly assist you to maintain your optimum health. Also, the same sound helps to open your Third Eye area. Do this exercise everyday for five to ten minutes. It does not really matter when you practice it, but, it would be more ideal to do this in the early morning.

## Sound Vibration Exercise for Strengthening Internal Organs.

Let me explain more about sound vibration exercise, expanding from the Ohmm sound. As I mentioned before, each sound has its own energy according to five different elements. Water energy has to do with the kidney; tree energy, the liver ; fire energy, the heart ; earth energy, the stomach; and metal energy, with the lungs. Each organ has its own particular vibration which strengthens it.

Let' s make a sound together. Feel your body when you make a sound. And, then see which part of your body responds to the sound.

Sound Ah···. You can feel that it vibrates around your chest area. The sound Ah··· is interconnected with the heart. It is a wonderful way to release the internal stress. If you feel uneasy, put your hands on your chest and make the sound Ah···.

Let' s make a sound I···. When you sound I···, you should feel the vibration from the sides of your trunk into the spinal area. The sound I··· is good for your stomach and liver.

In order to say U···, you have to strengthen your abdominal area. Thus, sounding U···helps you to accumulate the energy in your lower Dahnjon. Your kidneys and bladder will respond to the sound of U···

Now, with an exhalation, say, Huh··· your lungs will respond to this sound. Also, the sound Huh...will stimulate your stomach area.

S is the sound to stimulate your bladder. SSS is a sound to stimulate your kidneys.

As you will see, each sound has its own effects in relation to our internal organs. If your internal organ responds to a certain sound, it is the sound which vitalizes that internal organ. Therefore, these sounding exercises are wonderful ways to heal and energize your internal organs.

Once you can connect the sounds with your internal organs, visualize each organ when you create that particular sound. With visualization, the effect of sound vibration can be increased.

If you have any problems in one of your internal organs, practice that particular sound related to that organ. Imagine that your organ is healed and fully regenerated. For example, if you have a weak liver, focus on your liver and keep practicing the I··· sound. Imagine that the vibration of the I··· sound surrounds and heals your liver. If you sound it as a prayer to be healed, you will experience the amazing power of vibrational healing sound.

# C. Advanced Level of Brain Respiration Exercise

# E XERCISE 1

## BRINGING YOUR BRAIN DOWN INTO YOUR DAHNJON

Dahnjon means an energy center in our body. Dahn means red in Korean. It also means Ki. Jon means field, or center. Dahnjon together means the center of energy, or Ki—where we create, accumulate, and circulate our bio-energy.

There are seven Dahnjons in our body-three internal Dahnjons and four external Dahnjons. The internal Dahnjons consist of the upper, the middle, and the lower Dahnjon. The external Dahnjons are made up of two Jangshims on the palms of the hands and two Yongchons on the soles of the feet. We usually call the lower Dahnjon simply Dahnjon. It is located two inches below your navel and two inches deep inside your abdomen. Dahnjon is an invisible point, not an organ which can be identified through anatomy. If you keep practicing the exercises, you can sense it. For right now, you can assume that it is under the navel area.

### Dahnjon Breathing

Let's create a breath through Dahnjon.

For a beginner, a lying down pose is easier for practicing Dahnjon breathing. Once you get used to doing it, you can practice in a half lotus or standing pose. Lie down comfortably, and place your feet apart, about shoulder width. Your arms are at a 45 degree angle beside your torso, and your palms are up. Breathe slowly and release your tension through your fingertips and toes, while relaxing your body completely.

Now, let's begin breathing while adding abdominal movements. Inhale and extend your abdominal area outward as far as you can. Exhale and pull your abdomen inward, reaching toward your spine. Repeat this exercise several times. Do this breathing as naturally as you possibly can. Do not hold your breath longer than your own natural capacity. Just breathe as naturally as you can.

A baby in the mother's womb is breathing through the umbilical cord. Also, a newly born baby is breathing through Dahnjon, too. As such, Dahnjon breathing is a naturally encoded process of breathing. Now, imagine yourself as a child of the universe, as if you were in the cosmic womb. You have an umbilical cord on your navel which connects you with the source of universal energy. In each inhaling, you are taking in this cosmic energy through the umbilical cord.

Recovering Dahnjon breathing may not be very easy to practice in the beginning. Particularly, to breathe naturally while moving the abdomen, may take some getting used to. The important thing is to keep focusing your consciousness on the Dahnjon and breathe.

When you try to do Dahnjon breathing, you may feel uneasiness in your chest. Such symptoms have to do with the blockage of Immack, the middle line meridian of our body. In this case, you must practice chest breathing first.

Instead of Dahnjon, focus on your lung. When you inhale, expand your lungs as far as you can. When you exhale, let out all the stale air in your lungs. Your consciousness is focused on your chest during this exercise. On the inhalation, the energy comes down from your nose into your chest area. On the exhalation, the energy travels out from your chest through your fingertips. Practice this chest breathing about 20 minutes everyday for releasing any blockages in the energy paths of the chest cavity.

## Making your brain one with your Dahnjon

Once you keep watching your Dahnjon and focus your breathing, you can feel Dahnjon as a warm energy center. Imagine that there is an energy ball in your Dahnjon. The deeper your breathing goes, the larger the ball becomes. Soon you may feel that your abdominal area is filled by this fresh energy ball.

Through the imagination, bring your head into your Dahnjon. Gently put your head into your Dahnjon where now the clean and fresh vitality is fully recharged. Keep your eyes on your head inside of the Dahnjon and practice

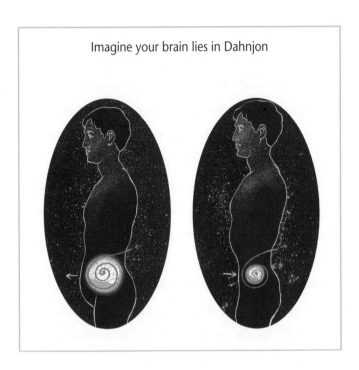

## Imagine your brain lies in Dahnjon

Dahnjon breathing. When you are inhaling, your abdomen is rising, while your brain becomes larger. With exhaling, your abdomen is contracted and the brain becomes smaller. Feel the unity of the movements between your abdomen and the brain. If you can keep a focused concentration, you can clearly feel that your brain is becoming fully alive and breathing naturally.

Imagine that your brain is inside of Dahnjon, like a baby inside the mother's womb. Your mind will stop its endless chatter soon, and you will experience the tranquil state where there is no thought or emotions. You have finally discovered the hidden treasure of your inner being, the ultimate peace. Your brain needs this kind of total rest. From now on, you can rest your brain in your Dahnjon anytime you need to experience this quiet peace. If you do this exercise, particularly before you go to bed, you can have a very deep sleep and will be fully refreshed the next morning.

### Visualizing a nose on the lower back.

You can either sit or lie down for this exercise. Relax your body and look carefully at your Dahnjon with your mind. Imagine that there is a hole in your lower back, exactly the opposite side of your navel. This hole is connected with your Dahnjon. We call this new energy point Myong Mun, which is a very important acupressure point in our body. Myong Mun means "the gate of life."

Imagine that this hole is a new nose on your back and that you are inhaling and exhaling through this nose.

When you inhale, the energy is recharged through this imaginative nostril, and vice versa. When energy is coming and going through this nose, it performs spiraling movements. Your abdomen rises when energy is comes through with the inhalation, and any tiredness is released when you exhale through your new imaginary nostril. Through this process, you will accumulate a very pure and fresh energy in the Dahnjon.

Once you get used to breathing with this new nose, again bring your head into your Dahnjon and continue taking a deep breath like this. Your head should feel light and refreshed. It is such a wonderful way to supply your brain with vitality.

### Ending the exercise

Now, slowly inhale and exhale. Take three deep breaths. Lock your fingers, push your arms over the head, then stretch as far as you can. Let the fresh vitality reach into each part of your body.

Rub your hands very fast to make your hands warm. Put those hands over your open eyes and send the warm vitality into your eyeballs. Massage your eyes with the fresh vitality from your hands. Now, wash your face and comb your hair with your hand of Ki energy. Do the same with your neck and then the whole body.

# EXERCISE 2 THE COSMIC DANCE MANIFESTED THROUGH YOUR BODY

Take a seat in the half lotus pose. Relax your shoulders and waist. Inhale and exhale, inhale three times. With each breath begin to feel your whole body get more relaxed. Make a prayer position with your hands.

Focus your awareness on the top of your head, Baeg Hoe. Call Baeg Hoe several times, in silence. Imagine that the most fresh and sacred energy is pouring down into your Baeg Hoe. Like a bright light, the crystal-clean energy is coming down into your brain. This light is illuminating your brain. See your brain, and feel each part of it.

Celestial energy gently vibrates the inside of your brain like a soft breeze. The vibration gets stronger, the movements of your brain grow larger, and finally, an intense vibration overwhelms your whole body. Now, you can sense

that your entire body is surrounded by this wonderful energy. Slowly your body starts to respond to the energy flow. Your neck, your upper torso, hands and arms want to dance with the flow.

Let the energy be in charge of your body. Without any particular thinking, simply go with the flow. Once you become accustomed to moving with this flow, your hands and arms will feel lighter and lighter, as if you are floating in the air. Like sea weed, your body is dancing in this cosmic sea of energy.

The movement from the flow of this universal life energy is beautiful. It is a never ending, creative dance with the cosmic energy. We call this Dahn Mu. Dahn means Ki, or energy, and Mu means dance. In short, it is a dance of Ki.

There is no instructed form in doing Dahn Mu. All you need is to follow your own rhythm and wave. You do not need to learn anything in order to experience Dahn Mu. Depending on the state of your mind, it could be slow or fast, calming or passionate. You may use your whole body, and could find some of your poses developing quite complex and delicate forms - something which is hard to experience from your outer consciousness. These graceful motions come from within your being, only when you are in that place of inner consciousness.

Imagine that you have become a rose in the summer breeze, or, a bluebird in the sky, a small and beautiful stream, or the void. You could be anything in your imagination. On a deeper level, you could forget yourself—your entire body, and become one with the void which is constantly moving.

In the middle of dancing, you will feel a deep joy and blessing overflowing from inside of you. You may experience tears, which is a good way to release all kinds of blocked emotional drives in your chest.

If you want to cry in the middle of Dahn Mu, do not suppress that feeling. Let your tears flow freely. After the tears, you will feel oneness with the whole universe in great peace.

### A Cry from the Right Side of the Brain.

When you do Dahn Mu, you will find a hidden dancer inside of your body. It is as if you have become an artist and can fully enjoy the happiness of creation. It is not a creation from the rational mind, but one from spontaneous inspiration. Through this experience, your hidden dancer feels a freedom which it never tasted before.

Once you practice Dahn Mu, the right half of your brain starts to work. Nowadays, people have more interest in developing the right half of the brain. Dahn Mu is one of the most interesting and easiest ways to develop the brain's right side.

Also, when you move your body according to the flow of Ki, your brain wave becomes more secure and calm than a quiet meditation. The deeper you can get into the subconscious mind, the more sensitively you will feel the energy you have become.

Dahn Mu is a naturally expressive way for your body to release any blockages. With all kinds of limited thinking and emotions, your hidden dancer inside has been a captive of serious mind, for too long. Let him/her express himself/herself through your body now, without any inhibitions. Let him/her be free.

As I explained before, Ki has the power of rehabilitation.

In order to balance and harmonize the energy flow of your body, Ki inspires you do all kinds of spontaneous postures and movements. If you have some pain in the shoulders, Ki may enable you to keep circling them. Through Dahn Mu, your inside energy is fully activated to penetrate the blocked meridians, and to correct dislocated bones. In short, Dahn Mu is a kind of self-healing process.

# EXERCISE 3    CLEANING THE NEGATIVE EMOTIONS FROM THE AMYGDALA

Seat yourself in a comfortable position. If you sit on a chair, place both your hands on the thighs. If you sit on the floor with a half lotus pose, grab your knees with your palms. Shake your shoulders and twist your waist to the right and then to the left. Get rid of any tension in your body. Again, sit straight and take a deep breath. Sweep down your energy field from your forehead, to the Dahnjon with your hand. Repeat this sweeping motion a couple of times, until you are totally calmed down.

From now on, you will do an exercise to purify the amygdala. Imagination itself is a brain exercise. When you use your imaginative power, you can experience deep breathing. Imagination is not simply imagination. It has its own power to manifest itself into reality. The only thing we need to do, is to accept that our imaginative world is just as real as what we call reality. Only when you believe this fact, will your brain be transformed.

With easy breathing, imagine your amygdala. You do not necessarily need to know where it is located in your brain. By simply imagining that part of your brain, it will

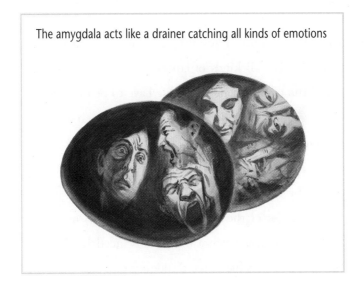

The amygdala acts like a drainer catching all kinds of emotions

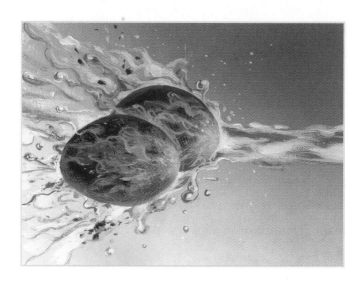

actually respond. The amygdala acts like a strainer which catches all kinds of emotions. Any emotions produced throughout your whole life have to be processed by the amygdala. Depending on your own self-imposed limitations, many kinds of emotions are freely passing through the net of the amygdala, while some are caught by it. Our emotional garbage is often captured in the dense net of the amygdala. Imagine this net in the amygdala. If you reach a highly advanced level of this exercise, it is possible to see through your brain and to see the amygdala.

Imagine that you are cleaning the filter of a water purification machine. In order to clean it, you tip the filter upside down and wash away the dirt. In the same way, you reverse the amygdala and pour the Ki shower on the net of the amygdala. See how the dirt around the net is washing out.

Then, through your imagination, prepare three glasses of pure water. Bring out your amygdala from your brain and dip into the first glass. Feel the coolness of the water in the cup and gently wash your amygdala with the pure water. Then, do the same procedure with the second and third cups of water. Imagine that the old memories which stick to the amygdala are being cleanly washed.

However, there may be some memories that we can't easily remove because they have stuck to the amygdala for too long a time. Now, prepare two more glasses of pure water to wash out persistent memories which have become the cells of the amygdala themselves. The first glass is named "forgetting". Soak your amygdala in the pure water of "forgetting". The dark memories begin to come out of the

Imagine all the emotional impurities in the
amygdala are being washed with the pure water

amygdala into the water by a kind of osmosis action.

The second glass is given the name "vision". "Vision" means a person's ideal of life. For the last time, rinse the amygdala with the water of "vision". Imagine your ideal of what you are like in that process. The highest vision in the universe is carved in the original amygdala not contaminated by anything else. It is "love" —a pure love for every living thing. You cannot entirely remove the emotional impuri-

| The Glass of "Forgetting" | The Glass of "Vision" |
|---|---|
|  |  |

ties from your amygdala until you wash it with the vision of "love". Watch the perfectly purified amygdala for a while, now that you are able to identify the original skin. And then return it to its position in the brain.

Now, focus your mind on the top of your head, Baeg Hoe. Imagine that a cool waterfall from heaven is falling down onto your Baeg Hoe. Your brain will feel so refreshed. Take three deep breaths. Concentrate on your Dahnjon and recharge it with your breath. Rub your hands until they feel warm, and then, massage your whole face and head with your warm hands. Open your eyes.

Once you start to practice this exercise, you may suffer a bit from all kinds of memories and negative emotions. Some forgotten memories of the past may appear on the surface of your consciousness. Particularly, your former traumas, or other terrible experiences may manifest, which you may have wished to not remember.

Our memories are all saved up in our brain as a form of energy. These affect our consciousness and our subconscious behavior. Even our past memories are also energy, in that simply remembering your sad experiences could bring some tears to your eyes. Unhappy experiences or negative trauma stay in your brain cells as a dark energy. Once you start to purify your amygdala, many of the memories you have elected to file away in your subconscious, may come to the surface of your mind. This is all part of the purifying process.

Therefore, even if your mind seems to lose its peace because of these interrupting memories, do not try to stop anything. Simply keep watching and let it be, as if you were watching TV or the cinema. After the purification, when your amygdala is clean and bright, you will not be bothered anymore by the negative thoughts. Only when you can detach yourself from your dark memories, will you be free from this self-imposed prison.

# E XERCISE 4
## BRAIN CIRCUIT EXERCISE

### *Brain Restructuring : Repairing and Activating the Energy Circuits in the Brain*

This part will introduce Brain-Circuit Exercise as a highly advanced level of practice for the purification of the brain. Brain-Circuit Exercise is a way to improve the energy status of the brain by using the picture of the Brain-Circuit, which is the geometric visualization of the optimal status of the brain. Circuit in this context means the form or shape of energy proper to each kind of object. Brain-Circuit, in this sense, is the visualization of the highest energy patterns of the human brain.

Everything in the world has its own energy pattern, the

circuit. The energy pattern imprinted in an object shows its own features, first, by the physical traits of the object such as shape, color, weight, and size. Hence there exist as many circuits, as there are shapes or colors in the world. The circuit, the proper energy pattern of an object, like the set of genes of a living thing, has individually distinguished features.

The energy pattern depicted by the circuit is not merely a geometric figure. The circuit itself has and radiates its own level of energy. For example, the circuit of a triangle has the triangular pattern of energy, and the circuit of a circle has its own circular one. Human minds are often classified, through geometric metaphor, into triangular, quadrangular, or circular ones. These also do not have merely metaphoric meaning, but they really show different energy patterns of human brain. Square or quadrangular mind is, though still angular, more tempered than the triangular one. When a person has tempered all of his/her angular or poignant elements from his/her energy, he/she will have a circular and generous mind.

The circuit is a visualization of a certain energy pattern

and itself gives off its own level of energy which is determined by the energy pattern it shows. The circuits are also different in the quality of energy. Some are pure and clear, (while) others are impure and contaminated. The circuits, though appearing to be fixed sets of pattern, are themselves moving ceaselessly and change the energy pattern of other objects by exerting some dynamic influence. Two different circuits, when placed close to each other, tend to be synchronized or assimilated. This is perhaps why they say "stay out of bad company". A person with a destructive pattern of energy can give very strong negative influence to the brain circuits of his neighbors.

Therefore, what matters most in doing Brain-Circuit Exercise is what kind of circuit picture one uses in the exercise. The circuit picture used in the exercise shows us the pattern of energy of the brain when it is in the best condition. Therefore the pictures have the power to restore the user's brain to the best possible state. For example, the Buddhist picture, the mandala, or the geometric figures or symbols of all ancient civilizations are that kind of circuit pictures, which show the highest level of energy. These pictures therefore have helped people in meditation for centuries.

The circuit picture leads the viewer to assimilate the energy pattern. The circuit picture of the brain in peaceful state leads the brains of those who are viewing it into the similar peaceful state. The people highly advanced in this practice can sometimes see the same pattern of aura. If some image emerges on the mental screen when you are in deep meditation, examine it closely and you will find it to be the same beautiful and symmetric pattern of an aura.

One can participate in the energy circulation the circuit picture depicts only by viewing it in tranquility and composure. Following the energy flow on the circuit will make the viewer's consciousness clear and the brain purified and optimized. Emotional turbulence makes one's brain swell, and the brain once swollen cannot be easily restored to normal condition. That kind of emotional turbulence hurts, most of all, the amygdala. The Brain-Circuit Exercise is the healing power for the injured amygdala and for freeing one's consciousness from the negative influence of the emotions. Following the lines of the circuit picture is the best and easiest way to liberate one's consciousness

# ■ Brain Circuit Exercise

Move your eyes following the lines of the circuits,
your can purify the brain and improve it's energy status
just by looking at The circuits. It is also recommended
to draw the circuits in the air with
a finger or on paper with a pencil.

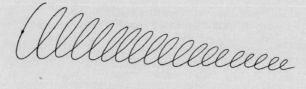

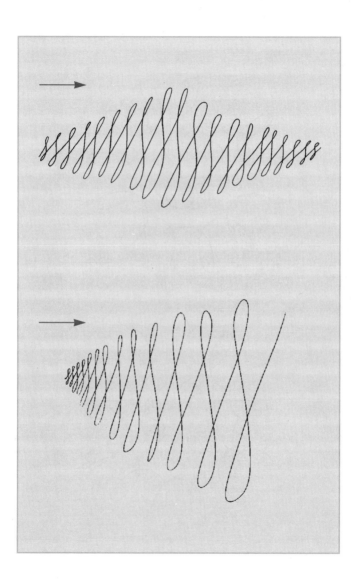

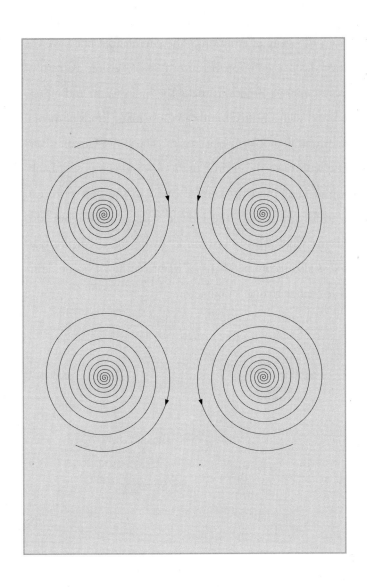

from the sway of emotions. The circuit does not have the least dash of emotion because it is the visible pattern of purest energy. Emotions make the brain warm and agitated, and such a heated brain can cause many kinds of mental or physical problems or diseases. The Brain-Circuit Exercise will make the excited brain cool and composed. Looking at the circuit picture of brain in the best state can transform not only the viewer's brain circuit but also his/her whole energy system. Drawing the circuit for oneself is also recommended as a way to bring the same desirable change to one's brain.

# D. Complementary Notice for Brain Respiration

### Two Common Healing Signs : Jin-dong and Myung-hyun

Practicing Brain-Respiration sometimes brings fundamental changes to one's body. One would be at a loss
when one meets the changes without some preparatory
knowledge about them. One of those special experiences is
Jin-dong, a kind of shaking, which comes when one is relaxed down into low brain-wave with clear consciousness.

It is similar to the phenomena which we can see when
you suddenly open a faucet and water under high pressure
begins to run through a hose: the hose will shake violently.
Usually the paths of energy inside the human body are half
blocked by stagnant, unclear energy. That problem is more
severe in the case of those who are obviously ill. But when

one learns to feel the energy, and the energy begins to flow freely into and through the body, the body will often shake violently as the blockades in the energy-path are cleared.

Jin-dong is divided into two kinds. In one case, Jin-dong comes when the energy is accumulated enough and is activated into rapid circulation. In another case, Jin-dong is made by the influx of the cosmic vital energy. The first case is possible only after a person has stored a certain amount of energy inside one's body, while we can experience the second case any time we open our minds.

Though one whose energy circulation system works well usually does not experience Jin-dong, everybody experiences, at any rate, some kinds of Jin-dong, the vibration of life. Everything is on its own wave and has its own peculiar vibration. In some cases, the vibration is so delicate that one cannot perceive it when one's body experiences Jin-dong. When one keeps on with the practice and some parts of our bodies are revitalized, even healthy people can experience Jin-dong.

Jin-dong comes continuously for a certain period, weakens gradually and completely stops. When one is in

Jin-dong period, one is easily too much interested in it. But if one is attached to the phenomena and has too much Jin-dong, it will make one exhausted. Because Jin-dong comes when one relaxes oneself and lowers one's brain wave, one can control the phenomena consciously. Jin-dong is a sign which shows that one's practice is ready to go up a level. One feels refreshed and pleasant after the experience of Jin-dong.

There is another healing sign as common as Jin-dong. It is Myung-hyun. Some people can be ill with cold symptoms as they go on with the practice. This happens as some obstacles in the energy path stop the flow of revitalized energy. It is a common experience that is inevitable when the increased flow of clear energy washes out the wastes in our bodies made by the stagnant and unclear energy. When one is in this condition, one feels as if one had a cold. This is the common manifestation of Myung-hyun.

The word 'Myung' in Myung-hyun means brightness, and 'Hyun' means darkness. Thus Myung-hyun has the meaning of alternating brightness and darkness, that is, periodically alternating change of our body conditions.

Through that kind of change, our body gradually proceeds to complete health. Therefore you don't have to worry if you sometimes experience repeated bad conditions while you continue your practice. Simply take it as a gateway you have to go through before you get to a much better state.

7. • Brain Respiration Results-
   3 Indivisual Experiences
• A Talk with the Author, Il Chi Lee

# 1. An Amazing Encounter with the Life-giving Light

*Jennifer Jones*

At the time I began to practice Brain Respiration, even a little walking made me short of breath as I weighed 160 pounds and am only 5 feet 2 inches tall. I was suffering from aftereffects of having a baby. After delivery of my first child, I developed a bean-size tumor in my womb. But I never went to see the doctor out of fear it could be cancer. Ten years went by in hesitation and fear. In desperation I tried several unconventional remedies. I took warm baths in boiled red clay or mugwort water expecting they would extract some deadly wastes from the body. For all the efforts, the tumor continued to grow and eventually, even sitting upright gave me much pain.

I was deeply interested in ways of natural healing and

Ki-exercise because I had all kinds of diseases over my body from head to feet. While I was looking for the proper practitioner or trainer of that kind of exercises, I saw an office titled Dahn Center and entered it (I don' t know why) without hesitation. I was impressed by the sight of people in meditation wearing white exercise clothing in bright light. I felt at home even though I had never been there before. Especially, I was greatly attracted to the master' s simple warmth and kindness.

When I had been practicing for three or four days, something stirred in me and tears began to well up and flow ceaselessly down my cheeks, regardless of my emotional state. This would happen even while I was driving or washing dishes, or before or after doing exercise. Those unstoppable tears caused me great embarrassment.

While teaching Brain Respiration, the master particularly trained me in intestine exercise. In intestine exercise, one repeats the motion of pulling one' s stomach backwards and pushing it forward to the limit. At first I did it two or three hundred times. After three days, I had bowel movements two or three times a day, and was cured of one of my chronic diseases, constipation. Now, I'm able to do the exercise one thousand times without trouble. Presently, when I come into a state of Brain Respiration after doing it one thousand times, I experience a kind of fluoroscopy and see the intestinal organs. Though astonished at the phenomenon at first, I have come to understand it as a process of my consciousness learning about my body. I believe that everyone has that kind of potential ability.

On the seventh day after I began practicing, I had a bowel movement that cleared the feces which had apparently been contained a long time in my intestines. It seemed as if my body became as light as a leaf and I felt like floating on clouds. Then a vaginal secretion began to ooze because, I guessed, the tumor in the womb broke. The bad smell of the secretion caused me to go home and change underwear as soon as I finished exercising. After four months had passed, the feeling of discomfort and heaviness disappeared and it seemed that everything to be cleared was cleared. Then I went to see the doctor and had an examination. Everything proved to be normal.

While I was going through all the changes, I lost 30

pounds. I welcomed this change not only for the sake of my health, but also, I loved my new figure. My skin became refreshed and shiny. Freckles and small wrinkles disappeared. I looked like another person.

Before I began practicing Brain Respiration, I felt my heart become more and more tightly constricted as I was continually gaining weight. I carried heart-medicine with me for an emergency since I had some trouble with breathing. Every night I went to bed only after taking medicine because I was afraid that I would never wake up again if I did not take it. Many times I fell into a coma while sleeping. I came out of it, in fortunate cases, after several hours in a hospital. In some bad cases, it was almost 24 hours before I came to myself. I often woke up to find my body swollen because my kidneys didn't work well. This condition caused pain on the soles of my feet while walking, or in my palm when making a fist. To make it worse, constant ear-noise made me unable to hear even the sound of the door bell.

I don't know exactly when and how I have become free from all of these maladies. My only secret is that I gave up all medicines and practiced the exercise earnestly following the master's teaching. I felt my body changing rapidly. After two months, I no longer experienced swelling.

A few months ago, I injured my spine by slipping down a stairway in my apartment. A lumbar vertebra was cracked and I could not move my waist at all. While doing intestine exercise, I felt a sharp pain as if my spine was strained and pulled apart. In those days, I got a chance to exercise Brain Respiration in an open field together with the master and other members of Dahn Center. When I was in Brain Respiration listening to the natural sounds of birds, streams, and wind, I felt the fresh energy of nature run around my body. It felt as if a hole was opened at the injured spot of the back-bone, and the natural energy came through the hole in the shape of a vortex. It made me feel refreshed and healed, and all of the pain suddenly went away and never came back.

In practicing the exercises, I found that I was cruel to myself by trying to be perfect and thus, I was too strict. This extreme perfectionism made my body and soul tired. Inability to take life as it is made me tense and robbed me of the relaxing pleasures in everyday life. Perhaps, the divorce from my husband made it worse. Up to now, I have not been familiar with my body, my mind, and the idea that I should love them. I have never cleared my heart of the inner story hidden in it. I have had only superficial contact with other people. Though that kind of relationship gave me no discomfort in everyday life, the undeniable feeling of loneliness was always around me. I have become interested in my inner life, my soul, for the first time since birth. I ask myself what it is I really want.

I often feel sorry about my husband and our failed marriage. If I had met Dahn, and Brain Respiration earlier, we could have led more matured married life. I pray for his soul that was devastated by my lack of consideration.

## 2. New Life on a Thirty six Year-Old Burn Injury

*David Lawrence*

Last October I retired from public life as a policeman because I had reached the mandatory age. While I was looking for some kind of proper exercise to refresh my body, I happened to see the Dahn center in the neighborhood. I began to practice the excercise the next day. I went to the center at 10 A.M. and 5 P.M. practicing twice everyday.

Three months after I began practicing the exercise, while climbing, I put my brain in my Danjon thru imagination, and did the breathing exercise - pushing the stomach forward to breathe in and pulling it backward to breathe out, imagining the brain was at Dahnjon all the time. When I took a step after finishing the breathing, I felt a pricking on my leg. I rolled up my trousers to look for the cause of the pain but I couldn't find it. There were no bites or scratches. The same thing happened the next day, too. The stinging pain I felt on my leg began to spread all over my body. Furthermore, red spots began to show up on the skin. Strangely the parts dotted with red spots were those I had scalded with steaming hot water in the bath years before. It seems that the scald revived itself 36 years later when the body was energized by Brain Respiration. I couldn't believe what was happening in and on my body. The red spots grew into blisters. The skin fell off and began to ooze. The blistered skin oozed so much that the bed sheet became wet in the morning. In addition, it smelled terrible.

That condition continued for more than two months and I was afraid. I didn't give up practicing, though. The training master said that it was just a healing sign that is natural and inevitable in the process of recovery. I trusted him and attended at least one session of training everyday. After three months with the affliction, the pain noticeably grew sharper and began to dry. After careful examination, I found that the skin was being renewed. The marks of the scald had all gone away again.

I kept on practicing Brain Respiration in the early morning. When I was sitting still in quiet and peace, my mind became free from everyday worries and the memory of my childhood showed itself in fresh visual images. It was incredible for me to visualize the long forgotten old days since a car accident that occurred two years after my wife and I had married, caused the loss of all memory of my childhood. And I suffered from absent-mindedness so much that I became worried about dementia. The Brain-Respiration seemed to restore the health of my brain and with that, my memory. In meditation, partial images came up on my mental screen and then disappeared. I met my mother and old friends in meditation,. How can I describe that kind of experience? My heart was full of happiness as if I been gifted with a new life. As I kept on practicing, my brain became fresher and my memory gradually improved. These days, I rarely make the sort of mistakes I used to make from forgetfulness. I feel like a teenager, both in mind and flesh, Practicing Brain-Respiration changed my personality a lot. Nobody will find in me the blunt and quick-tempered old policeman. The most pleasant thing for me in practicing the exercise is that instead of always receiving energy from others, I now can gather energy myself, and move it in my body or give it to other people. The visitors to the Dahn-center usually have some problem with their body. I can understand them and their troubles better than anyone else, and thus, I'm anxious to give them any kind of help within my ability. I feel happiest when I see people who came in frowning, go out smiling. I cannot find words to tell you how happy I feel now that I can love those around me as well as my own self.

## 3. School-life is Happy

*Betty Gates*

I used to be rather reserved and shy, losing confidence easily and not really knowing what to say when I had to talk about my ideas before other people. I felt I was weak and small, and wondered if I could be helpful in any way to others. Most of all, my mother's death last year was such a tragedy for me that I hardly had any interest in my everyday life. I refused to be in intimate relationships with others for I didn't want any more parting tears. My father worried about me so much that he suggested that I go to a gym for some exercise. But I didn't want to do that.

One day, a friend of mine brought me to an open class in a Dahn-center. What impressed me was Dahn-dancing, a free representation of inner feeling which is possible when a person becomes one with the natural energy. That was the most beautiful sight I have ever seen. Something sticky I felt while practicing the basic course of Brain-Respiration also gave me some mystic pleasure. I felt at ease in the center though I couldn't tell why. After two months of practice, I no longer felt abandoned and discouraged. I began to enjoy meeting people.

The person who was most pleased with the changes in me was my father. Before those changes, I didn't talk much with my father and easily became angry with the smallest problems. When I changed, everything around me looked different. My school life changed, too. Anytime I felt tired at school, I practiced a few simple motions I learned at the Dahn center. Sometimes I even spontaneously massage my friends on their heads to make them feel refreshed.

I used to feel it was difficult to concentrate, but after a few weeks' training in Brain Respiration, I can easily focus my consciousness on anything I want. I intend to practice harder and be able to teach my friends at school what I learned about Dahn and Brain Respiration.

# A Talk with the Author,

## Il Chi Lee

*interviewed by Hale Dowksin, President of*
*Sedona Training Associates*

....Thank you for taking the time to give us this interview. There are many possible styles of life even in a small cultural unit, and the range of choices is becoming wider especially in a highly developed and modernized society like United States. But very few people choose it as their life purpose to find the ultimate meaning of their existence. Will you explain what it is inside you that made you decide to go for enlightenment and freedom?

---

■ Hale Dowksin, president of Sedona Training Associates, interviewed Il Chi Lee on the enlightenment and his book, Brain Respiration, at Dahn Tao Center in Sedona on the 16th of June, 1997.

**L :** When I saw, while working in a hospital, that the patients once thought to be cured come to see doctors again and again, I could not help asking what would make people lead truly healthy lives free from cares and diseases. Their problems were not theirs alone. They were also mine. I kept asking what causes disease, cares, pain and death and what I could do to solve these fundamental problems. After a long period of searching, I came to the conclusion that all of the problems have their roots in the depth of human existence itself. I wanted to reach to the core of existence and find some final truth, if any, that gave an answer to all of the questions at once. What I wanted exactly was, as I found later, not just truth. It was some really practical way to bring myself and other people enlightened. How many of us can follow the examples of Buddha or Jesus to get enlightenment? This explains why I took the path from body through mind to the Real Being. What I met, or rather what visited me on the way was the cosmic energy, Ki. Ki is the basis of all existence and phenomena in the universe. It is the inexhaustible source of life.

Disease is, in short, a state of being cut off from the flow of cosmic energy. Then, how can people get cured from their disease, mental or physical, except by coming back and becoming one with the true source of their vital energy? Being cured is, in a sense, a small acquisition compared with other blessings they will get from enlightenment. They will meet their true being, One Self. It means rebirth. They will take it as their life purpose to be beneficial to the whole mankind.

**H :** I think such a special experience as enlightenment would be the most dramatic turning point in one's life that one can ever get. How did you experience life before as opposed to the life after enlightenment, what is the difference?

**L :** The difference is not on outside. Enlightenment, of course, can bring some changes to the physical state or facial expression of the enlightened person. But a more important and radical change is in his/her view or perspective. The view is unimaginably widened and the perspective is limitlessly multiplied. The paintings of Picasso may help as one visualization, though simplified, of the way an enlightened person looks at the world. Our True Self can be anywhere and everywhere, anytime.

How can I define myself? My body, my ideas, my habits, my senses, my emotions, my desires,···no matter how long the list may be, it cannot contain 'I'. Even the synthetic total of the items is not 'I'. They are mine. I'm the master of all those things. I am Ch'on-ji-ki-un and Ch'on-ji-ma-um, that is, cosmic energy and cosmic mind.

**H :** As you know, love is the central theme in Christ's message. But I don't think it to be just a principle for practice for us. Rather, it seems that he wanted to show what kind of power is or should be dominant in the cosmos. What do you think the role of love is in enlightenment?

**L :** Heaven and earth are always making love, ceaselessly producing all kinds of life. Sung-tong, a Korean word for enlightenment means literally a perfect communication, which is the consummation of love. Any loving people who have ever experienced that kind of communication will not forget the great joy they got from totally being one. Imagine what the joy will be like if you can have such communication with Heaven or the whole cosmos.

Of course, on the other hand, love is also a principle of practice for us. Maybe, it is the most appropriate word to describe the energy which an enlightened person has. It is, I think, after enlightenment that one realizes exactly what love means. One's feeling in enlightenment may be the highest level of happiness. As for me, nothing was more precious than the joy and peace I found in myself and nothing was brighter than the divinity in myself. At first, I wanted to leave this world as I didn't want to have that kind of perfect blissfulness contaminated by any other worldly experiences. I considered going out of this flesh by controlling my breath and heart beat. But after a while, I came to think that leaving this world like that was a kind of ingratitude, considering the grace I had got from Heaven.

Willingness to go the thorny way, even if it leads to death, as we see in the example of Jesus, that shows what love means for an enlightened person. Enlightenment cannot be kept as a personal experience. It was not 'my' experience for there remained nothing like 'I' that would like to claim possession over that experience. My decision was to share my enlightenment with as many people as possible. The decision was not so easy as it sounds because even an enlightened person, in the material level of existence, can not avoid being involved in various forms of conflicts and struggles. When I was thinking what I should do, I heard a message from One Spiritual Master. I felt an irresistible responsibility for the betterment of our world and its residents. What I was given then as a code to decipher the secrets of the cosmos was Ch'on-pu-kyung, an ancient holy scripture which had long been waiting to be understood

**H :** My teacher, Lester once talked about struggling with himself over a decision like the one you mentioned; whether he should go or stay. He also felt responsible for other people and took it as his duty to help them get free from their cares and anxieties. Coming back to your story, was there any special sign or experience you had right before enlightenment?

**L :** Enlightenment is an instantaneous visit of cosmic energy and heavenly wisdom which nobody can expect or anticipate. Or rather, I had no time, no mind to read any such signs because all of my energy was concentrated inwardly. As I knew that enlightenment was not such a thing that I could choose on my schedule, I brought myself to the extreme of existence, to the verge of life and death by not lying, not sleeping, not eating for 21 days. I had to walk around to stay awake. Even I stood for three days holding a pine tree in my arms. I fell off a cliff three times while sitting there in order not to fall to sleep. I felt an unendurable pain in my head as if it were about to explode. I thought I would die from the explosion. A strong desire for my security came over me. When I could not stand it any longer, I left everything, including my life itself, to the hand of Heaven. At the very moment, I heard a big bang in my head. I thought it had been blown off. Then suddenly, a great peace came to me and all of the pain disappeared. I could see the cosmos in myself. There were no inside, no outside. I could understand what Buddha meant when he said "I am the only One in the Whole World."

**H :** I heard about your new book, Brain Respiration, if I remember exactly. I felt the title was quite interesting. Can you explain what is brain respiration?

**L :** I got the basic ideas about brain respiration from the big bang experience at the moment of enlightening. It seemed that two parts of the brain which had long been disconnected were suddenly brought into unity by an enormous energy, under extreme conditions. It was that the circuit in my brain had become repaired, and an original connection restored. The same thing can happen to anyone and through the recovery of connection, one can replace one's self in the fundamental order of life which cannot be reached while one is kept within the walls of false 'I'.

But the problem was who would do what I did, for something, though claimed to be good, as questionable as enlightenment? I had to find some easier way for my neighbors to follow. That is why I made and refined the ideas of brain respiration.

**H :** I understand why you think it necessary to find some easy way, but I can have no clear idea of brain respiration yet. Is the title metaphoric or practical?

**L :** When asked how one breathes, anyone will say "with lungs". But "lungs" merely points to the place where the gas-exchange occurs. What occurs in breathing is not only gas-exchange. What is more important is energy-exchange. One can have it happen anywhere one wants in one's body because energy flows along the path of one's consciousness. Where your mind goes, there goes energy.

Breathing is usually divided into three kinds ; thoracic, abdominal, cutaneous. However, as you know, what controls all the organic functions in one's body is the brain. Thus, one cannot experience a perfect energy-exchange if there is any blockage of the energy flow in one's brain even when one's body functions well in every part. This made me look for some simple and effective ways to repair the circuit in the brain. One of them is to draw repeatedly the symbol of infinity($\infty$) on one's mental screen. One may draw it with one's body because one's bodily expressions have their own images in the same energy patterns as one's brain. Brain respiration is, thus, a way of breathing to make the brain integrated by repairing the circuit of energy in the brain.

**H :** As far as we know, our brain is the place where all of the information we have got through our life is stored and where all of our mental activities are taking place. We think consciousness itself is a state or a function of brain. Then, I can't help wondering who or what controls the brain.

**L :** That is a very important question, and it is related to the ultimate purpose of brain respiration. If one keeps practicing brain respiration, one will have some day a sudden contact with the True Controller, the true 'I'. The enlightenment will come like an unexpected present. It is a remarkably easy and integrated way to get there, and this is where Dahn Hak differs from other methods of discipline. One practical method based on brain respiration, Vortex Dance, will show what I'm saying. It is an integrated form of discipline, including bodily exercise, breathing, meditation, and dancing. Imagine attaining enlightenment while one is dancing in joy. How exciting and encouraging it is! The idea that the way to enlightenment is only along ascetic penance is quite misleading.

**H :** Lester too structured the method with intention to help people realize their true being. But he knew also people are what they are and had various needs for wealth and health. Thus he helped them in many ways to get those things. He wanted them to get through those things to enlightenment.

**L :** There are many paths to enlightenment. What is more important than enlightenment itself is to make one's enlightenment real in practice. I have thought about this for a long time and what I have been doing since enlightenment is mostly concerned with that. Unless one makes one's life conditions compatible with one's enlightenment, or makes one's life itself an enlightened one, the brightness of enlightened consciousness may lose its light and fade out into darkness. Thus, in Dahn School, enlightenment is the starting point, not the goal. It is after one gets enlightened that one needs a teacher to guide one's spiritual growth. This is because even an enlightened person has to carry one's body and the body has many habits or tendencies acquired from the life before enlightenment. Most of them, contrary to one's will, are resistant to the drastic changes, mental or physical, one's enlightenment brings. This is why I have thought some training courses are required even after enlightenment.

**H :** Do you think, then, everyone has to go through that kind of training course after enlightenment?

**L :** Enlightenment can be divided into two levels. The energy one experiences in the highest level of enlightenment is so powerful and perfect that all of the previous tendencies including habits, desires, and emotions are completely burnt up. One who obtained enlightenment at this level is literally a freshman. There remains nothing to bind or direct the person into a certain fixed set of behavior patterns. Any action the person takes is his/her spontaneous choice and clear expression of the inner voice. But most people cannot jump up to that level in one bounce. They will experience enlightenment at the second level. They also know what enlightenment is and what incomparable joy it gives, but they are still partly in the old tendencies, which have a force like a gravitational pull on them. Unless they are transformed through a process of purification, that force pulls them back into the old track they once left. The brightness and joy of enlightenment becomes just a good memory of good old days.

Enlightenment does not mean some superhuman power. An enlightened person is one who does what anyone can do. What is beyond human ability is also beyond an enlightened person's ability. It just shows the person that he/she has a unlimited potential power in himself/herself. It can be compared to a high-tech computer system. Whatever great capacity it may have, it means nothing more than a tin-can if the owner does not know how to make effective use of it. In order to make the person do that, he/she has to be given a task which needs the best of his/her ability and wisdom. It is when one uses the maximum of one's energy that one grows. Thus, enlightenment is, in this respect, a ceaseless breakthrough of one's own limits.

**H :** The image we usually have about an enlightened person is like that of a hermit. Therefore I was a little startled to hear about the way you live. You seem to have wider range of interests, from meditation to business, than any other person, whether enlightened or not. This makes me curious about what you have done after enlightenment and what you want to do for our future.

**L :** This is a really tough world for an enlightened person to live in. At first I thought that I could make people enlightened by sharing my experience, but some of them called me a liar or a lunatic, and others asked me what was enlightenment good for. I remembered the remark of a great enlightened person that a prophet rarely gets honor in his own country.

Realizing that they were not yet open to what I wanted to say, I modified my course a little and started from one of the most universal subjects, health. Who will not care about it? I began to teach people exercise in a city public park. I wanted them to feel the energy flowing through their bodies. While doing so, I met more and more people and took some of them as my pupils. Since the first Dahn center opened 13 years ago, increasing numbers of people have begun to practice Dahn Hak and now, we have more than 360 centers in and out of Korea. I came to the U.S 3 years ago to have wider communication with people in the world.

Wider communication, as other good things do, has its cost. The more connected I become with worldly affairs, the more uncomfortable I feel. Sometimes I miss those days when I could be in meditation without any disturbances. It is not really an easy job to be an enlightened businessman.

Nevertheless, I'm still trying to find some easier way to lead more people to enlightenment and freedom. Brain Respiration is one of the results of the effort. I have a vision to enlarge the circuit explained in Brain Respiration beyond individuals to such a scale as to hold the whole world and all people in it. On the basis of that kind of global network, people can have, in the literal sense, total communication with each other. I take the task as a game, and really love it because it requires us to play with our best energy and wisdom.

## *Dahn Center in U.S.A*

| | | |
|---|---|---|
| Ahwatukee 480-783-4885 | Annandale 703-658-6440 | Ballinger 206-366-1122 |
| Bellevue 425-373-9959 | Beltsville 301-595-2056 | Boulder 720-565-0609 |
| Brea714-990-3550 | Brookline 617-264-4851 | Centreville 703-266-5363 |
| Chicago 773-539-4467 | Clark 773-755-9566 | Denver 303-694-2717 |
| Duluth 678-475-0405 | East Meadow 516-227-0101 | Flushing 718-762-6373 |
| Fremont 510-979-1130 | Fullerton 714-994-1306 | Garden Grove 714-537-3499 |
| Glendale 818-265-9356 | Glenview 847-998-1377 | Great Neck 516-487-8406 |
| Harber steps 206-223-9642 | Hawaii 808-942-0003 | Irvine 714-669-8330 |
| Las Vegas 702-256-6778 | Littleton 303-795-8622 | Manhattan 212-725-3262 |
| Marietta 770-971-1171 | Memorial 713-464-7012 | Mesa 480-464-9068 |
| Olympic 213-381-3893 | Ridgefield 201-941-8622 | Rockville 301-424-9033 |
| Rowland 617-264-4851 | San Mateo 650-577-0321 | San Francisco 415-752-0800 |
| Sanjose 408-241-0328 | Santa Fe 505-820-2211 | Schaumburg 847-882-6980 |
| Scottsdale 480-391-8916 | Sedona 520-282-3600 | Somerville 617-623-3246 |
| Syosset 516-364-3413 | Torrance 310-791-0301 | University Way 206-524-7166 |
| Valley 818-343-6960 | Vienna 703-242-9373 | Wall street 212-791-2442 |
| Waltham 781-647-7733 | Westmont 630-230-0365 | Woodside 718-205-4435 |

C.G.I Holistic Fitness Club 201-768-8845
Sedona Retreat & Healing Park 520-204-4403

## *Dahn Center in Canada*
| | | |
|---|---|---|
| Beaches 416-686-5492 | Bloor 416-530-0947 | Mississauga 905-281-3467 |
| North York 416-630-3157 | | |

## *Dahn Center in Japan*
Tokyo 3-3358-2753    Osaka 6-6765-5699

## *Dahn Center in England*
London 776-149-4399

## *Dahn Center in Brazile*
Sao Paulo 11-223-6460

Majo Garden 5∽ -625-2256
Sedona